NEW SHAPES OF REALITY

by the same author
FOR YOU THE WAR IS OVER (PETER DAVIES)

NEW SHAPES OF REALITY

Aspects of A. N. Whitehead's Philosophy

BY

MARTIN JORDAN

———

London
GEORGE ALLEN AND UNWIN LTD
RUSKIN HOUSE   MUSEUM STREET

PRINTED IN GREAT BRITAIN
in 11 on 12 Juliana Type
BY SIMSON SHAND LTD

FOR MARGARET

CONTENTS

INTRODUCTION

The first book I ever found by Alfred North Whitehead was in a prisoner-of-war camp near Sulmona, Aquilla—a setting since immortalized by Ignazio Silone with *Fontamara*. Our camp lay on a slope of the Appenines where it was all rotten rock with grass. A monastery, always dark and silent, stood on higher slopes. At our level they had built the civilian penitentiary, and in the valley the villagers lived in the upper stories of houses, the ground floors being for the family animals. America had not yet entered the war; there were no free allied troops in Europe. The atmosphere was not exactly claustrophobic, because one could see a vast spread of country under clear skies; but all the things which could be seen—clouds, dust and the shapes of trees—somehow took on the human faculties of being bland and inscrutable. This was because of the total lack of information about the war, which would otherwise have given our scenery a context.

The book referred to was a Pelican edition of *Adventures Of Ideas*. In those days it was possible to own all the published Pelicans and store them on a short shelf. A Pelican—it went without saying—was a book from which the intelligent layman could grasp the latest state of the sciences. Readers neither expected nor received more than this; a Pelican was what one read for the facts, and the facts, for example, were of genes, crystals, radiation or archaeology.

Adventures Of Ideas was a long book with terse chapter-headings, like 'Beauty', 'Peace'. At first the style seemed merely *dense*. A tendency of the reader to rush through the coppice of a paragraph would quickly be arrested by tendrils of phraseology and reduced, if not cancelled. But such tendrils as these mentioned were not adjectival or superfluous; the shock of slowing up in the reading, as often as not, lay in the power of *nouns*. One realized that certain words were being made to perform in regions strange to their field. A term of physics would hang together in a sentence with the vocabulary of the arts, or something boundlessly vague would suddenly acquire the status of a living organism. In time, of course, it became clear that this was a habit of generalizing so refined that each example stirred with novelty. If that were not so, in a particular case, the effect was still of insistence towards cliffs barely glimpsed and the anticipation of vertigo as on approaching an edge.

It is certain that I did not make sense of *Adventures Of Ideas*. However, I signalled through the Red Cross for some key, some explanation, and soon London University sent *Whitehead's Philosophy of Organism* by Dorothy Emmet. This was not a Pelican, but a book with hard covers; and as the authorities did not admit hard covers, for fear that compasses, maps or currency might be hidden between the boards, I received Professor Emmet's work in the form of two hands-full of loose pages.

After that the war caught up with Sulmona Camp, and I doubt if I thought about Whitehead until 1947, the year of his death. It was the year in which I read *Science And The Modern World*. I remember noting that the odd sensations of reading him rootlessly in a prison camp were not being repeated.

When we hear of the late Sir Thomas Beecham complaining to Lord Boothby that there was too much counterpoint in Bach and protestant counterpoint at that, we are reminded of the story of Bach's obituary in which the composer figured as 'the famous organist'. We are left to ponder the subject of posthumous reputations. J. S. Bach was an artist who stuck to old-fashioned liturgical form in an age of musical transition. Turning to western philosophy, we find ourselves in a comparable age: Wittgenstein its Mozart, Alfred North Whitehead its Bach. When he died after the Second World War, in the odour of the Order of Merit and with his sheerly philosophical Harvard period behind him, there were many who thought of him as a mathematician.

This book may appear to pose at times as an exposition of Whitehead's philosophy, but really it is more of a personal account of the impact of Whitehead on one reader. I expound, and in some instances discuss, various features of his philosophy in the most untechnical language I can muster and within the tentative spirit imposed by my own limitations. The purpose is to assemble some of his main ideas in such a way that the reader may be tempted to go further—perhaps to read books of greater authority, such as those listed in the bibliography, and then start

on Whitehead's own works. Most of the books about Whitehead are expositions, explanations or critical assessments, but the
present work—I repeat—does not pretend to be any of these; it
would be more accurate to compare it with autobiography; and
it is aimed simply at the promotion of enthusiasm in others. Like
all writers I have tried to visualize the typical member of my
audience, and I see him, or her, as fairly young, not unacquainted
with general philosophy, but not so well advanced that hard
attachments have formed. In other words, I am not pretending
to myself that this book is likely to influence a middle-aged
Oxford analyst. On the other hand, if any be on the road to firm
opinion, I would like to feel that this book could tempt some
into Whiteheadian studies on the way, for if it is good to have an
open mind, Whitehead of all philosophers offers the best
encouragement.

In its rôle of mere introduction to more technical studies, the
book has been presented as a literary essay without footnotes. It
is in two parts. The first expounds, with an approach that is
often more journalistic than technical, prominent features of
Whitehead's philosophy; the second deals with his particular
approach to metaphysics and contains more of my own views on
the subjects raised in the first part.

A word about Whitehead himself. He was born in 1861. His
father was a vicar in the Isle of Thanet, England. As a mathematician he collaborated with Bertrand Russell in producing the
standard work *Principia Mathematica*. From an appointment at
London University in the twenties he went to live in America at
the invitation of Harvard University, where he became Professor
Emeritus. His philosophical works, as opposed to those of his
books which are mainly concerned with scientific subjects, nearly
all date from the Harvard period.

I would like to thank Professor Dorothy Emmet, of Manchester
University, for her helpful criticisms and great encouragement.
I am also grateful to Dr Edmund Burke, of Reading University,
for much solid help in the task of understanding Whitehead,
especially on the side of logic and language. There are passages
in the book which owe themselves entirely to his presentations.

PART ONE

CHAPTER ONE

INTERRELATEDNESS

1. OBJECTS AND SUBJECTS

Many readers feel that Whitehead's books amount primarily to a criticism of the assumptions of classical empiricism and scientific materialism. He had no finished alternative to offer when he began the enterprise; his 'final' scheme (the inverted commas are used because Whitehead never in practice admitted finality) was formed gradually in the course of a long life. What emerged was a new basis for the understanding of nature and the worlds of common experience—art, religion and physical science.

Man is an individual, and his strongest impression of the universe is that it consists of *self* and *not-self*. There is Tom—that is, ourselves—and there are all the things which are not Tom. If we perform a familiar feat of mental athletics we are able conceptually to stand outside this situation and see Tom as a subject for the world's impressions, and the world itself as a complex of objects affecting Tom. We call this wider view an object-subject relation.

But in managing the intellectual leap which enables him to see himself as subject and the world as object, Tom is nevertheless making himself one of the objects. Whenever he names himself —'I'—he is giving himself the status of an object. The true subject, the organism called Tom which is doing the thinking, is a much more slippery customer.

When it comes to that type of philosophy which tries to clarify the kind of universe that not only surrounds but *includes* Tom, the evasiveness of Tom himself becomes a hurdle at the outset. It seems clear that Tom, the subject, is what he is *because* of the objects—the rest of the universe. The fact that he wants to philosophize, unlike Dick who wants to learn botany, is owing presumably to the effect the universe has on him personally; and he cannot *consistently* interpret the universe in terms other than personal, however 'objective' he tries to be.

Obviously this division of the universe into subject and object could be carried to logical absurdity. No one, in fact, qualifies every statement with 'It seems to me' or 'As far as I'm concerned'; few are solipsistic enough to hold factual remarks like 'the cat is in the cupboard' to be without meaning except as items of auto-biography. But empiricism has often in the past been subjectivist in tone and has tended to accord statements about experience this limited sense and to deny universality to most things that are said. Science, on the other hand, seeks ideally a world that can be described and predicted in independence of the observer, and where the observer tends to obtrude (as in some branches of physics) is concerned to expel him as best it can. Empirical philo-sophers like Bertrand Russell (and Whitehead himself in his earlier work) gave thought to the problem of how to 'construct' the public world of science out of the private world of experience. In general the solution offered by western empirical philosophy was to 'sack the subject', to remove Tom altogether, except in those instances, such as psychology, when he is necessarily to be treated as object. Out of that decision physical science, with its immense utility, had arisen. But the cost had been heavy, amount-ing in our time to no less than the widespread abandoning of metaphysics as a possible study. For if in the nature of things the universe cannot be examined or explained until it has been simplified into a collection of objects, independently existing and made up of substances with qualities, then the function of philo-sophy must be negative. It must confine itself to explaining why any knowledge of an alleged reality behind appearances is impossible, and to the criticism of attempts to profess such knowledge.

One of the more controversial of Whitehead's activities as a philosopher was to affirm the validity of metaphysics. His criti-cisms of the familiar world of 'objects'—the world dealt with by commonsense and physical science—are so thorough that they seem at times like a return to a Periclean spring. Christianity and the scientific renaissance never happened. We fancy our-selves to be back with Plato and Aristotle and to be starting afresh from there.

The result is radical, to say the least. Beginning with the well-known doctrine of empiricism, that knowledge is a matter of experience *via* the sense organs, and that ideas not firmly based on such can tell us nothing about reality, we straightway part company with the empiricists. For what philosophers like Newton, Locke and Berkeley then tried to do, Whitehead would maintain, was to postulate all sort of things, in themselves not experienced, which were supposed to be *causes* of experience. These were the familiar entities of science, such as sound waves, light rays, the motions of molecules, etc. The consequence was that the sights, scents, noises and other firsthand experiences of Tom were not the universe after all. The universe was something different, and only appeared to Tom in the guise of sights, scents, etc., because Tom possessed a mind and physical organs. In any description of the universe Tom's propensity for having experiences could be left out. The agitations of molecules that caused fire were real. The fact that Tom experienced, not agitated molecules, but a private and incommunicable feeling called hotness, was irrelevant.

Whitehead puts back Tom's feeling of hotness by insisting on the data of *experience* and only experience. To the task of analysing and co-ordinating that experience must be brought the main tools of philosophy, reason and generalization. Experience is 'the self enjoyment of being one among many, and of being one arising out of the composition of many'.

This is not to say that either pure or applied science have in any way failed; on the contrary, they are spectacularly successful. Nevertheless Whitehead sees science as a *department* concerned with the description and measurement of pieces of the universe that have been abstracted forcibly for the purpose from a totality of things that includes Tom's private experiences. Thus science as we know it should not be mistaken for a mirror to reality. It is more like a blueprint. As a description of a cathedral an architectural blueprint is useful. But what about the sensation in the hands when you touch a stone and wonder how many have done the same? What about the smell of incense, the play of dark and coloured light, the almost tangible weight of religious feeling? Such thoughts easily suggest that science is but *one* thing in experience: that the task of seeing wholes can belong only to philosophy.

In his books one sees the growth of Whitehead's opposition to a philosophy which carves up the universe into independent lumps. Nature, Whitehead insists, is interrelated. There is an equal rejection of theories which give supremacy to 'things' and their qualities. Closely linked with this clearing of the ground is the refusal of modern philosophy in general, and of Whitehead in particular, to recognize the traditional logical doctrine which gave the subject-predicate form of judgment precedence over other forms.

Such ideas will be examined later. One result of their application is Whitehead's analysis of experience.

Experience involves a relationship. A mind, one might say, is required to be present, and things for that mind to perceive and think about. It seems probable that the mind is what it is *because* of the things it has perceived or thought about. But as we have seen, that is not enough; for mind becomes an isolated substance, qualified by its experiences, and the universe is crammed with unconnected things—tintacks, motor cars and individual minds. Mind, says Whitehead, is not passively affected by independent objects *but is essentially related to the object it perceives*. This is a difficult notion. We have done our best to present it as simply as possible in the following chapters.

When we consider *what* is presented to mind in experience we find a queer state of affairs. The universe as experienced by mind and its attendant sense organs is an overpowering impression of sights, sounds, tastes and tactile feelings. Basically these impressions are all we have. But no one who has been brought up on science will feel comfortable in saying that the impressions 'are' nature. A sensation in our ears, coupled with another in our noses and reinforced by a third in our eyes, is not the English Channel. Everyone would say that the English Channel is something *other*, something which gives rise to the sensations; although the means are quite complicated, being concerned with light waves, sound waves, titivations of the olfactory nerves, etc. The sensations are the *appearance* the sea assumes. We know it to be 'really' something else. The titivations of our nerve-endings are best understood by calling them 'apparent' nature. The real things, which do the titivating, should clearly be called 'causal' nature. Apparent nature is mental. It is nothing without sense organs and minds. But causal nature is simply 'there'. It has nothing to do with minds. The English Channel would go on heaving and splashing if every mind in the universe vanished tomorrow.

The above is unquestionably the attitude of commonsense and science. It is also the view which Whitehead attacks above all other. He will not allow any division of nature into apparent and real. Nature merely means what is given in experience. The hotness we feel as we sit before the fire is as real, and as much a part of nature, as the mental experience we have when we read that the hotness is 'really' caused by agitated molecules and heat quanta.

If there is no 'apparent' nature, then the sense-impressions we have are nature itself. They are not the appearances of some underlying realities we can neither see, smell or touch. But on such a view does not the familiar world seem to dissolve? For sense-impressions are surely experiences of the qualities of *things*. Behind the qualities the thing-in-itself must somehow be lurking. An apple is round, cold, hard and red, and it has an apple-like smell. Most people are convinced that there is something in addition which is not just coldness, hardness, redness and a scent of apple. What is it? Lamely, the reply must come— 'the apple'. Even if the universe were a completely interrelated system, surely the most fundamental relation of all must lie between substances and accidents; or in logical terms, subjects and predicates; or in ordinary speech, things and their qualities! If these were not the basic relations between parts of the universe, in terms of which most other relational situations can be explained, an alternative must be proposed, and it had better be good!

Whether one accepts it or not, Whitehead does rather ingeniously produce the requisite alternative. Although it may be a useful way of thinking for day-to-day affairs, he says, you are led into impenetrable mystery, philosophically speaking, if you analyse creation into things-plus-qualities—ships (tall), shoes (shiny), sealing wax (red). Before you can hope to resolve inconsistency you must analyse experience in a different way, taking as the bricks or standard units, not things but *events*.

In this view our ideas of subject-object, and of things and their qualities, become at best but useful abstractions. Below the level of such ideas there exists a primitive 'brick' of creation, the event or occasion, which Whitehead calls his *actual entitity*. Within this small slab of space and time we find united subject and object, percipient and perceived—all opposites and irreconcilables that have been the despair of metaphysics. The Whiteheadian event is a 'becoming' or self-creative process. It is characterized by *feeling*. Within its terms Whitehead manages to analyse not only the complexities of the organic body, but also spacetime and religion.

2. 'PRESENTATIONAL IMMEDIACY' AND 'CAUSAL EFFICACY'

One of Whitehead's criticisms of classical empirical philosophy has to do with the problem of determinism, involving cause and effect. The topic is always interesting, and most people at some time have been drawn into argument about 'free will'.

Whitehead did not believe in a mechanical or materialist universe. Such a universe would consist of the 'mere hurrying of material'—a hurrying, moreover, at the behest of mechanical laws—causes and effects. There would be no room in such a universe for free will because every event would happen as a result of compulsions which would have to be described ultimately, not truly in terms of experience but in sets of statistics. The universe of Newton is the house of determinism. As Laplace pointed out, if someone knew enough about events to mark everything that happened up to a given moment, the materialist must allow that such a person could foretell the future. Everyone in his view would appear predestined. The fact that such a being could only be God is not necessarily enough to make a Newtonian universe at all endearing! That the achievements and failures of mankind are in basis illusory is of all ideas the most repugnant; and this would apply even if the nature of things were such that people had to act *as if* free will existed.

As Whitehead's philosophy, in the pursuit of interrelatedness, modifies in a striking way the traditional view of cause and effect, it will be fitting to pose the question so often discussed: do we possess free will, or is life confined to the tramlines of predestination?

A phrase spoken many times by a British army at war is 'If it's got your name and number on it, you've had it.' Many tend to be fatalistic when bombs and bullets are around. It is customary at other times to assume a will that is free. Few worry on the score of inconsistency. Danger—an air raid warning, the thunder of bombs—is an alchemist which distils determinism in a trice. In the bomb crater, or the trap of a flooded submarine, physical causation is the only principle of nature which seems to make sense. In such circumstances it is possible to accept *Hamlet* as the complicated result of biochemical frolics in Shakespeare's glands—to fail to see any qualitative difference between being a man and writing a poem and being a stone and rolling downhill. But when the battle recedes, or hawsers start to lift the submarine, the erstwhile determinists relapse into comfort—are prepared to reject all notions of a totally mechanical universe. In practice a world where you can neither praise nor blame is intolerable.

Determinism, one feels, is useful enough for scientists but a bore and a bugbear in other fields, for instance in art. A chemist would be entitled to smile if someone suggested that the reactions between his substances were brought about spontaneously by inspiration. Yet few think that mechanical laws, abstractions reducible to mathematics, produced the Jupiter Symphony.

To the artist, mechanistic explanations are acrid. But the scientist is unconcerned with acridity; neither is the maker of fertilizers concerned about the smell. If you want the product you must put up with it; and if the world needs effective science, accurate weighing and measuring and consistent patterns of nature, it is convenient to assume that everything that exists, once it had been thrown by some deistic hand into a pre-created receptacle, retained no option as to its subsequent history—it simply *had* to become what we see around us. Perhaps, so potent is causality, a bear which coughs at the North Pole stirs the sands of the Sahara, and the following limerick is not altogether *nonsensical*:

> There was an old man called O'Rory
> Who rightly maintained *a priori*
> That morning vibrations
> Of freight cars in stations
> Did something to *Alpha Centauri*.

Some years before the Second World War, certain popular works by the physicists, Sir James Jeans and Sir Arthur Eddington, brought comfort to many. These suggested that science had lost faith in the mechanistic thesis and suspected the universe to be less like a slow combustion engine—more like a thought. People began to talk with gratitude about the principle of indeterminacy in nature. But war clouds were gathering, and the universe hardened again and became more physical. When you might have to kill somebody it seems possible that your actions *could* have some effect on Indian elephants and the spiral nebulae. On the other hand, when you *think* of something—anything, Falstaff, the Moon, the left foot of Woodrow Wilson—you cannot believe that the mere thought could affect the universe in any way.

Is mankind compelled to behave *as if* free will existed? Many would hesitate to include subjective feelings in the laws of nature. It is a fact that some do not demand free will at all. Einstein was content to give mechanism a clear field, from the path of a comet to the lighting of his pipe in his sitting room. Nevertheless, many western minds find the need for freedom deep-rooted. Few escape their moments of puzzlement about the bifurcation of nature that is apparent to thought, the barrier where matter ends and abstract values begin. Beauty and justice live on one side; stubborn and inexorable fact—'the hurrying of material'—on the other. Neither seems qualified to visit the territory of the other.

Perhaps it is to intuition that we should turn? For example, the following from Santayana:

'To omniscience, the idea of cause and effect would be unthinkable. If all things were perceived together and co-existed for thought as they actually flow through being, on one flat phenomenal level, what sense would there be in saying that one element had compelled another to appear?'

However, an intuitive vision such as this is inclined to dissolve when we break our shoelaces.

As will be seen, Whitehead tries to account for the duality of freedom and compulsion in experience. Meanwhile, there is a recurrent human illusion to be noted—that experience seems to suggest free will for the person having the experiences, but determinism for persons being experienced. Where the causal structure of everything seems obvious, the observer alone is poised in unruly freedom. Few *habitually* see themselves as machines; they are aware too strongly of choosing, willing, making mistakes. It is the 'man next door' who exhibits deterministic laws. His choosing and willing are nauseatingly mechanical. Even his incursions into novelty fall under suspicion. 'Why did he do that? It's not a bit like him. Is he drunk? Is he ill? There must be *some* reason.'

In fact, you are not living him; you are observing him. In Whitehead's account you are an historic route of events or occasions. The man next door is something stubborn and immovable that has cropped up in one of the occasions.

An occasion is the *now*. It has already perished as a concrete actuality while the last sentence was written. From the occasion —*now*—we gain all our impressions of freedom; it is this, in Whitehead's phrase, which 'ever-plunges into the creative advance'. Behind the occasion in time there is mechanism. One event follows another; the repetitive element in change is basic to thought. But the occasion itself departs from the pattern to make room for judgment, the will, the perils of responsibility. Like a wave it repeats its fellows, but on its crest it bears the novel and the unpredictable.

To return to the topic of causation, it will be wise to consider the character of *predictablity*, which at first sight seems to point to the interrelatedness of causes and effects. The problem of determinism has always been of interest to laymen; and everyone is a layman outside his speciality. But the scientific issue is not one of determinism. The physicist is unconcerned as to whether the reign of cause and effect is absolute or not. His daily care is the capacity of science for predicting events. When Laplace upholds the theoretical possibility of predicting the whole course of events from the universal situation at a given instant, the scientist would reply that all this is too impractical to be of interest. But perhaps it is not impossible to make statistical predictions about *large numbers* of entities or particles, if not about individual ones?

As it is often possible to make such predictions, the preoccupation of the physicist is directed to predicting the behaviour of smaller and smaller samples. He does not care whether the movements of material are determined by past events or whether the universe 'has' freedom; his time is too much taken up with hard truths like the fact that by no technique of observation is it even theoretically possible to find both the exact position and velocity of a particle and hence to predict its adventures with unlimited accuracy.

Is this because the single particle is 'free', an erratic individualist? That again it is impossible to know, even in theory. For if we had some unimaginably sensitive instrument through which to observe the particles, their behaviour would be affected by our act of observation. The weight of our microscope's illumination—the tangible beam of light—would kick it around like a football.

In his *Treatise of Human Nature* David Hume made some celebrated remarks about cause and effect. This relation or connection between objects, Hume pointed out, is the only one that can lead us beyond the immediate impressions of our memory and senses. We can enjoy *feelings*—pleasures and pains—but if we wish to go beyond the immediate experience and draw an *inference* from one thing to another, the idea of cause and effect is all that is available to us. How does the idea arise? From experience, says Hume, which tells us that particular things, in every instance of which we are aware, have always been joined with each other. Here is one of these things—say the sound of a motor horn—and we presume at once that its usual attendant exists; we look sharply for the car.

This account, Hume maintained, was unquestionable. But what does it involve? It means, Hume continued, that probability is founded on a presumed resemblance between things of which we have experience and others of which we have none. When I hear the motor horn I entertain the probability of the car. The sound is something of which I have just had direct experience; the car is something of which I have none. In fact I may discover that there is no car; it is a boy tooting an old-fashioned motor horn which he carries in his hand. Such an incident might bring home to me that I have been *presuming* the usual attendant, the car. My presumption is wrong. But on reflection the whole idea of cause and effect turns out to be a similar sort of presumption, and we habitually found our notions of probability on such presumptions.

As Whitehead points out, the criticism arising out of Hume's account has never properly been met. Let us see what is involved, taking another familiar example—the action of a magnet on iron filings. We might say that whenever the magnet approached the iron filings certain definite events followed, and that these were somehow *necessary* and not the result of chance or coincidence. Perhaps we might add that there is a 'power' or 'force' exercised by the magnet which causes movement amongst the iron filings.

We can *see* no power or force; all we see are the magnet and iron filings and that the proximity of the one to the other always leads to certain events. So we decide that there is an inevitable connection between the effect (the movement of filings) and the proximity of the magnet (the cause). All we can truthfully say is that the one happening is always seen to follow the other. The law of cause and effect that we have drawn up as a result of this observation is our way of trying to account for the habit of one kind of event to follow another. But there is only one proposition, says Hume, which is either intuitively or demonstrably certain from our situation. This is *not* that something is caused by something else. It is merely that the same principle cannot be both the cause and effect of another.

Observation cannot find the 'power' in the magnet; all it finds is the iron filings being influenced. Perhaps *reason* tells us that the power exists? Reason, alas, gives no such assurance. The fact that iron filings act in this way is not necessary. It is necessary that 2 + 2 and 3 + 1 are equal. The convulsions of the filings belong to a class of facts which 'happen to be so' and, for all we know, could be otherwise. If we were born into a universe where iron filings *changed colour* on the approach of a magnet our reason would not in any respect be violated; soon we would pretty calmly be noting that particular feature of nature. On the other hand, the thought of being born into a world where 2 + 2 did not equal 3 + 1 is an immediate threat to reason.

A necessary fact presupposes a continuing state. If 2 + 2 equals 4 today, it is of the nature of things that such will continue. Causation tells us that certain things have been conjoined persistently in the past; one cannot be quite sure that they will continue. Science finds new effects and modifies old causes.

Four is not different in essentials from 2 + 2. It *looks* different, but a child would say at once that it is 'really' the same. The child is right. Four is a tautology. On the other hand, an effect is *totally different* from a cause. There is nothing in the flame of a match that resembles the scraping of the head against the side of the box.

There is nothing like Beethoven's Ninth Symphony in the turning on of the radio. If these are separate events there can be no connection between them. If, as commonsense says, there *is* some sort of connection, they are not separate events.

We see a pile of ashes. We say, 'There has been a fire.' If our purposes are practical, e.g. we are insurance investigators seeking evidence of arson, we are luckily exempt from metaphysics. 'Either there is something about the immediate occasion,' Whitehead complains, 'which affords knowledge of the past and future, or we are reduced to utter scepticism.' The events of experience must be rescued from the predicament in which Hume has placed them if we are to claim theoretical knowledge from their patterns.

Whitehead's operation of rescue consists of his doctrines of 'presentational immediacy' and 'causal efficacy'. There was a time when a philosopher, in popular thought, lived best in a hermit-like isolation, in case the universe proved too much a distraction from his thinking about it. The modern alternative is to be implicated in the universe as much as possible. Whitehead would have maintained that the paths of implication, primarily, are the capacities of organisms for having feelings. Our sense organs are not unassisted in this. The immediately apparent character of sense-perception is its immediacy. Nothing in raw experience lies outside the moment of presentation; unassisted by overtones of consciousness, it has no references beyond itself. It is a shock or tingle and nothing more. But the tale cannot end there; for how in that case could sense-perception be so rich—so effective in shaping the individual and society? Whatever gives the richness must lie apart from the mere signallings of sense organs.

As telephonic receivers for presented experience, our sense organs, in themselves, do not say that the present is derived from the past; neither do they add that the present conforms, whilst still the present, with the shape of the future. This is the concern of feelings other than the five senses.

Some of our experiences are unassisted by these transforming feelings. Such are loosely described as unconscious feelings. A woman is reading an absorbing novel and paying no attention to the tap above the kitchen sink which needs a new washer. Drip! Drip! The sound had no meaning for her. In retrospect she may recall it as part of her animal condition at the time—the lines of print, a heater warming her knees, and the persistent drip—but whereas the matters conjured up by the book fill her with echoes of past and future, the dripping tap is a meaningless feature of the present. Then she finishes the book and begins to feel irritated by the tap and to construe ideas of washers and plumbers. The dripping tap passes from something presented in immediacy—raw and insignificant—to something sufficient for understanding the past and altering the future. Unassisted, the senses presented raw immediacy. Helped by the bodily feelings they gave efficiency to causal distinctions, performing the 'sorting out' which makes sense of our experience.

The bodily feelings are neither solely nor necessarily intuitive. In raw immediacy the separate messages of the senses are clearly marked. Intuition is not eternally standing by with glue to bind them together. It is something else that stands behind the bodily feelings, giving a context to events and piling the stuff of memory. This is best described as the whole make-up of the individual considered as an organism—the oneness of mind and body. Intuition is not bound up with the situation to the exclusion of other activity, but is that exercise of consciousness which involves, not physical objects and senses, but ideas—propositions. The dripping tap is a physical experience and gives our subject the idea of plumbers. She decides not to call for Jones. Jones, she reminds herself, has not the reputation of being a good plumber. Our subject has now experienced a proposition. A mental construction is launched involving Jones, his past reputation and probable future, finishing with the intuition that Jones might someday be forced out of business.

This brings us to an important feature of Whitehead's philosophy, and one that will be encountered again when we come to discuss the nature of an event or occasion. The lady in our illustration experienced the dripping tap as a raw happening, and neither Hume nor Whitehead could find any connection between that happening and the inference that the tap needed a new washer. But Whitehead added another concept. From what he called 'presentational immediacy' the bodily feelings of the lady moved to a kind of savouring of the situation which involved elements of past and future. This general apprehension of the experience offered by the dripping tap is in the mode of what

Whitehead termed 'causal efficacy'. The Classical empiricists had seen the sensory body as a receiving station engaged in the interpretation of *signals* of the type of 'shape + colour + scent = Rose', and it took a David Hume to point out the impossibility of deriving necessary causal relationships from the signals. It may seem astonishing that no philosopher went further than this until Whitehead advanced the notion—in retrospect, it seems, so obvious—that a being with sense organs *feels* itself as such, and that it is this efficacy of the total organism which gives feelings of causality as opposed to the mere presentation of given data to inference. We propose to return to this topic when we come to discuss Whitehead's account of perception.

An appeal to everyday life entirely confirms that sensations or sense-impressions are experienced *in themselves* to a most significant degree. A person may have blue eyes and light hair, but these are seldom experienced as blueness and lightness without further references. Their interplay is cumulative and emotional and has a regard to past and future. On the other hand, a *camera* would receive the impressions in the mode assumed for mankind by classical empiricism. So, to a significant extent, would a creative artist engaged in 'seeing'; and obviously the same mode would be applicable to a scientist carrying out 'observations'. But the mode does not apply to the more common act of living.

The example suggests a further advance into the thickets of Whitehead's philosophy. It might seem from the terms of the occurrence that the mind of the lady who contemplates the dripping tap is engaged in imposing its conditions on the things offered to consciousness by the everyday world. This would coincide in general with a type of metaphysics suggested by the system of Kant. But such a system would involve more than one level of 'reality' and offend against Whitehead's preachment of interrelatedness. A few Kantean examples might make this more clear.

If one assumes the universe to be in basis orderly, the further assumption would seem to follow that logic and mathematics must of necessity emerge as finished sciences from its study, because they would be imposed on minds by the recurrences of nature. But such an explanation takes no account of the *a priori*. There is a tale of Plato's about a slave whom Socrates forced to prove a geometrical theorem by appealing to reason. The ability of the ignorant slave is explained by a theory of reincarnation; it is held that the slave remembers something learned in a past life. More than 2,000 years later Kant advanced a more plausible theory of how we seem to have a modicum of knowledge without learning it. The idea of reincarnation is rejected, but so is the theory that logic and mathematics are thrust into our minds through the orderliness of nature. Any thrusting to be noted in the situation, Kant held, is that of the human mind itself.

We are bidden, in this view, to see two aspects of creation, the one open and the other closed to sense. The open part contains the ships, shoes and sealing wax of everyday perception. This aspect, says Kant, is an abstration from the whole. It has been made willy-nilly by minds because their structure compels them to make it. They have been formed to digest certain ideas only, just as animal metabolisms are adapted for certain kinds of food. Fed with the raw data of the senses, they go on to 'work up' the data into conventional ideas. But the total world from which the ideas, as it were, are compulsorily selected, is beyond human scope. It cannot form part of science; it is a closed aspect of creation.

Consequently we can have no absolute knowledge of an object—say a hammer—but only of those physical sensations which, collectively, are recognized as 'hammer'. But there are sensations different in kind from the physical, i.e. moral feelings. Many principles, such as 'Thou shalt not steal', seem to claim universal qualification. Such are held by Kant to afford a degree of contact with the closed aspect of creation—the 'real' world beyond the range of the physical senses. The marriage between subject and object which the mind, with its built-in limitations, could never achieve, is attained at last by the moral sense.

So when someone says 'This hammer is hard and heavy,' he is speaking, not of the real world in its totality, but of an abstraction which the mind had made compulsively. On the other hand, if he had said 'The hammer is Smith's: I have stolen it, and I should not have done that,' he would have been saying something about reality in the total sense. The key lies in the word 'ought'. 'Ought' figures nowhere in the scientists' scheme. Psychology examines what a mind wants to do, not what it ought to do. Physiology studies the mechanism of choice, not its subject-matter; conscience defies dissection. But it is precisely conscience,

says Kant, that is more actual than anything else. It is the ampli-
fier of the voice of the real world from the depths of moral nature.
It belongs to that world. The sphere of lesser reality—of measurement, number and spacetime—searches for it in vain.

If the mind makes an abstraction from the 'real' world for its
own purposes, it is implied that an occasion of experience is a
construction of some kind. Whitehead agrees wholly. Where he
parts company with Kant is on the nature of the thing constructed. According to Kant it is an objective world, manufac-
tured out of the experiences of the subject. But Whitehead insists
that the *subject itself* is the thing constructed. This sounds incredible; the subject under construction is myself—Smith, Jones!

Kant would have said that the lady who construes ideas of
washers and plumbers from the dripping tap is an example of
mind imposing its conditions on the offerings of nature to consciousness. But in Whitehead's account, the mind— the experiencing subject—arises from the world which it feels and *builds
itself up* out of its contact with an occasion of experience. This
most difficult of notions is made even more formidable, at first
glance, by the fact that Whitehead invented a new word to
describe it as an element of process. The world is 'prehension',
and it will be necessary to define it in later chapters.

3. 'SIMPLE LOCATION' AND THE BIFURCATION OF NATURE

'Simple location' is a supposed character of matter whereby it is
to be found somewhere in the universe existing at one time and
in its own way without any relations with other pieces of matter
in different places or at different times. Whitehead points out
that this presumed character of matter was the foundation of
classical physics. He adds that among the primary elements of
nature presented to experience there is no element which, in
fact, has this character.

In spite of much movement in science to the side of relativity,
'simple location' is still the instinctive world-view of most people.
It offers refreshment to commonsense, because the universe *looks*
precisely like a collection of things 'simply located'. The grammatical usages of civilization are geared to it; such familiar
concepts as 'there', 'not-there', 'that' and 'this' perform com-

fortably in such a context, and it is most difficult to imagine the kind of structure language would need if it were geared to some alternative context. One might say that our practical lives depend on this view of nature, for it is hard to think of anyone being pedantic enough to repudiate common terms and daily references on the grounds of their metaphysical inadequacy. Nevertheless, this view of nature has helped largely to give rise to the well-known 'insoluble' problems of philosophy.

The commonsense view that nature consists ultimately of pieces of material extended in space is immensely important as an existential convention. By its means we can go about our local and humdrum transactions with a minimum of bother. But it is no more the *only possible* world view than Euclidean geometry is the only possible geometry.

What Whitehead does is to present an analysis at odds with 'simple location'—one that might almost be said to involve a new syntax for thought. It will be salutory to remember, however, in the following pages, that nature, or the features, recurrences or 'laws' with which science deals, may be seen just as legitimately against a background of 'simple location' as that of Whitehead's system. It is nowhere claimed that his analysis is more than a consistent presentation of experience. It does not compete with science; you cannot weigh or measure a point of view. His ideas are not meant to be displayed this way or that in any sense measurable to science. He presents different logical spectacles with which to see nature. He claims that certain problems have seemed insoluble up to now only because the spectacles provided by 'simple location' were inadequate.

The system of logic or grammar one adopts as a backcloth for the appearances of nature or the events of experience must always be arbitrary. The appearances themselves might be illusory, or mistaken in detail, or misunderstood in their relations; but they *cannot* be arbitrary. It is impossible to choose whether to be burned or not when one places a hand on a hot saucepan. What one can choose is to regard the burning as an accident, or a punishment from God for some crime, or a moral lesson to teach us to be more careful in future. Thus Whitehead's philosophy is more of a speculative scheme of interrelation than a discovery of anything measureable or countable.

Of equal importance with his rejection of 'simple location' is

Whitehead's celebrated contention that 'science bifurcates nature into the sensed and the postulated'.

There is a fence down the middle of the universe. On one side are ideas—sense-perceptions, intuitions. On the other are the 'things' that give rise to the ideas. Science says, 'The one is appearance and means whatever you want it to mean; the other is reality and just is.'

Atoms are beyond direct observation. When one is contacted there is a remote electrical effect which is what the atom offers by way of appearance, and this is a subjective and psychological reaction to something postulated as an atom. On the one hand we have 'our' territory with its special probes and windows of psychological time, space, perception and feeling; on the other lies the domain of the mysterious reality called an atom.

It is this reality behind the phenomena of physics which Whitehead calls a 'hurrying of material'. Apparently it is into this that the mind projects the myriad qualities—hotness, colour, softness—which make up the sensed world. 'Thus,' says Whitehead in a much-quoted passage, 'nature gets credit which should in truth be reserved for ourselves: the rose for its scent: the nightingale for his song: and the sun for his radiance. The poets are entirely mistaken. They should address their lyrics to themselves, and should turn them into odes of self-congratulation on the excellency of the human mind. Nature is a dull affair, soundless, scentless, colourless; merely the hurrying of material, endlessly, meaninglessly.'

How is the trap to be avoided? We *can* usefully regard the appearance as the individual experience of something outside the observer. But we must include the experience itself in our estimate of nature, rejecting the idea that the universe is 'really' something else. 'Our experiences of the apparent world are nature itself,' says Whitehead.

It will be clear from the above that Whitehead is resolute in expressing revolt against the division of nature into dual systems of 'reality'. Yet precisely this, he maintained, is the scheme offered by science. There is (a) the world as known to the senses with its enjoyments of manifold impressions, and (b) the world of quanta, particles, waves, etc., discussed by science. The scent of the flower, the sound of the fanfare, the taste of the chocolate—these are directly affairs of the senses. But the entities of physics have little available to give to the senses; mostly the senses do not know them. This topic lies at the centre of Whitehead's philosophy.

The *modus vivendi* of the scientists' scheme is that the duality complained of does not exist, that we are only imagining two systems of reality because we mix up mental with physical concepts and causes with effects. Thus it is bound to sound complicated if you try to express your enjoyment of natural scenery in terms of light-waves. Senses belong to the minds of people and animals, and it is nonsensical to imagine them existing apart from the people or animals. What science does is to deal with whatever exists *apart* from the senses—with whatever can be said to be the *cause* of the sensory experience. When a person praises the scenery in front of his eyes he is praising the way his optic nerves received the impact of light-waves impinging upon them at 186,284 miles a second.

The above may certainly be characterized as a mode of explanation, the item explained being the impression afforded an organism by its sense-organs. In the same mode, however, must be included the mythological account of things in terms of gods and demons 'pulling strings': fever wastes the body of the unfortunate tribesman, but the *reality* of the situation is the rage of the tribal god whom he offended. The inadequacy of the explanation is made the more obvious by such terms; yet the mode of explanation posed by the following from Galileo is scarcely more satisfactory than the rage of gods:

'. . . The thing that produces heat in us, and makes us perceive it, which we call by the general name fire, is a multitude of tiny corpuscles, thus and thus figured, moved with such and such a velocity . . . and I judge that if the animate and sensitive body were removed, heat would remain nothing more than a simple word.'

The dilemma which Whitehead has tried to approach may be stated as follows. We can try to explain objects (a) in terms of their sensory, aesthetic or ethical qualities, or (b) in terms of the physicists' system of 'corpuscles', etc.; but the residual puzzle is how anything explicable in such a range of terms can be a single thing.

To take one of the alternatives—the explanation in aesthetic terms—let us imagine that the object we seek is a beautiful woman. The explanation will be one of innate qualities or virtues and in all probability will involve a teleological account of cause and effect. Such an explanation is of a type from which poetry arises. '*Her warm heart is washed with noon.*' '... *A phantom of delight.*' '*Steel-true, blade straight* . . .'. Such expressions, in which poetry delights, imply an underlying reality—a cause of the effects the woman has on us—which is of the same order as the feelings and emotions she inspires.

In the last—the scientific—alternative we are bidden to note statements about entities removed from direct observation—entities about which we have no marked feelings, which do not smell, taste or make noises, and of whose very existence our knowledge depends on the intellectual operation called inference. Electrons, atoms and molecules bear no resemblance to a beautiful woman, or indeed to anything except their fellows. We are told that the requisite quantity of these must amount exactly to the woman under discussion, and that there is no part of her that is not entirely made of them. The account would doubtless deal with the various convolutions of the entities, and how they combine into groups in getting 'built-up' to make the woman. But there is a point when explanation ceases and we have to say, 'Ladies and gentlemen, behold the result!' and draw back the curtain that conceals the woman. The connection with what we have been talking about and the woman as encountered perforce by our brain and senses is simply not present. We might have been talking about fishing or stocks and shares—there seems as much relevance between the warm and actual woman and those pursuits as between her and the subject-matter of physics.

Such seems the penalty of claiming a special status of reality for the mathematical properties of objects. The seventeenth- and eighteenth-century scientists who started this activity would have distinguished sharply between the 'apparent' woman, all rosy flesh and psychological overtones, and the 'real' woman expressed in the physical formulae. They would have spoken of the former as being caused by the latter. In a sense the lady herself would be an illusion, or at the least a lady without claim to existence in her own right in the absence of a mind available to tot up the atoms and molecules and thus respectably vouch for her existence.

But it is the woman, after all, who is given in sense-experience. Science claims to be grounded in experiment: what is proposed must be verifiable, must 'work'. In the last analysis the accounts of electrons and wavular patterns must be placed alongside the woman and shown to be the *necessary* causes of her marvellous effects. For if statements about electrons, etc., concern a world wholly removed from experience, are they not as mythological as the offended god who sends fever to the tribesman? Would it do any more violence to reason if it were held that the woman is born of Zeus, or fashioned of light and air, or formed from Adam's rib? On the whole, it is not difficult to join with Whitehead in holding it a retreat from empiricism to say that experience is a subjective adventure springing from a 'real' universe of electrons, etc.

In short, Whitehead insists that the simple electronic events at the microscopic end of things, no less than the finished experiences of a conscious mind, are *both* living exemplifications of nature itself. To a classical empiricist such a doctrine would have seemed, at the least, unscientific. No strict empiricist could have accorded the status of reality to anything in nature unavailable to observation and experiment. In the Whiteheadian view, the first need for empiricism is to establish the status of the senses and bodily feelings as an agency for creating the future out of the past, for it is on these that it finally relies. But the empiricists made a prodigious leap without noticing it, from living experience to the scentless, colourless world postulated as the 'reality' behind it.

Newton proclaimed that 'our business is with the causes of sensible effects' and when experimental evidence was lacking he would 'frame no hypothesis'. He saw the task as one of generalizing from sense-experience rather than seeking 'occult' principles behind it:

'To tell us that every species of things is endowed with an occult specific quality by which it acts and produces manifest effects is to tell us nothing. But to derive two or three general principles of motion from phenomena, and afterwards to tell us how the properties and actions of all corporeal things follow from these manifest principles, would be a very great step in philosophy, though the causes of those principles were not yet discovered.'

In this view, to explain scientifically is to show that the phenomena in question follow from general principles, i.e. are instances of recurrent patterns of events in nature, such as Raindrop—Clouds—Saturation Point—Fall in Temperature. This is the only sort of explanation we can offer when we postulate no other connection between events than observed sequence. The cause is then no longer pregnant with the effect: it is merely prior to it. And when we 'explain' a sequence all we do is show that it is familiar.

We do not say that a mother is merely prior to her child. To be part of a sequence of cause and effect means primarily *having feelings* about the other members of the sequence rather than mathematical relations with them.

Newtonian physics required the notion of absolute space, time, etc., a requirement now abandoned in the theory of relativity. Absolute space, time and motion are efficient instruments for bifurcating the universe; and as pointed out above, much of our ordinary thinking, in spite of the new climate in physics of indeterminacy and relativity, is still anchored in the sheltered bays of classical mechanics. From such a haven the universe is a concourse of 'simply located' material, set in the receptacle of empty space and 'being itself' through a universal flow of time. All the bits in the concourse have qualities (length, breadth, height, speed, etc.) and a 'natural process' means a change in these. To quote Whitehead:

'Only one mode of the occupancy of space is allowed for—namely, this bit of matter occupying this region at this durationless instant. This occupation of space is the final real fact, without reference to any other instant, or to any other pieces of matter, or to any other region of space.'

The significant point of the classical scheme to our present discussion is the lack of reference of one thing to another. Whitehead continues:

'. . . if in the location of configurations of matter throughout a stretch of time there is no inherent reference to any other times, past or future, it immediately follows that nature within any period does not refer to nature at any other period.'

The 'simply located' material object is supposed to persist

through time. In that case, we may ask, what is change? The answer would be that the electrons, etc., do not change; what we call change is their different configurations from moment to moment. In that case 'change' would have nothing to do with the primaeval particles as such; they are fully described by their properties at any instant.

As the atomies are pieces of *matter* (or more strictly, matter-energy) and presumably have nothing mental about them, it is easy to draw from the above the classical idea of 'substance'—a notion much older than seventeenth-century science, and one connected, rather, with Aristotelian logic. Substance is that which is 'in itself' existing in independence of everything else. The explanation that arises from this definition is in terms of general principles of connection. We can discover no link between the behaviour of atoms, on the one hand, and electrons, on the other, in any sense comparable with the behaviour-patterns, say, of mothers and children, or between one phrase of music and another, or the demands and responses of lovers; all we can do is note that there are recurrences of behaviour and try to frame Newton's 'two or three general principles'. The result is a purely descriptive physics, always telling us *what* but never *why*. Or as Whitehead magnificently puts it, 'a sort of mystic chant over an unintelligible universe'.

Science can, and does, of course, try to tell us *how* we come to experience the world as we do, *how* the colours, sounds and tastes are related to the actions of the light waves, etc., on our organs and nervous systems. We know how we come to get quickening pulses at a certain passage in a Beethoven quartet. It is a matter of frequencies, auditory overtones and intervals. If our minds were not present the quartet would be marks on paper. If performed automatically on tape in an empty house it would be waves in the air. Presumably the waves would be there if every inhabitant of the country had fled to Antarctica; presumably, therefore, the waves are 'reality' in a sense not shared by the music, which must be the appearance the waves assume when they collide with eardrums. The only possible commentary on this account, which in itself is unquestionably scientific, is that we do not buy record players for making waves in the air.

Thus Newton and his contemporaries hastened the bifurcation between the private and public worlds, between the sensed and the postulated. The problem felt keenly by Whitehead was that of reconnection and the subsequent exhibition of the universe as a process involving all experience with the feature of interrelatedness. It is true that many western minds, with the exception, probably, of some Marxists, are able to recollect a personal retreat from materialism or mechanism within the course of a lifetime. There is more 'in' life, it is felt. Whitehead attempts to replace something vaguely felt with a coherent analysis of the whole of experience.

To do justice to the Newtonian approach, it should be recalled that seventeenth- and eighteenth-century thinking was still dominated by the logic of Aristotle, including the classical analysis of judgment, i.e. that each can be reduced to subject-predicate form—to *judge* being to affirm or deny a predicate of a subject. It is a doctrine rejected by modern logicians, its best-known critic being Bertrand Russell. The most obvious method of criticism is to produce examples of judgments which cannot be reduced without distorting their sense, and these have been found in abundance in numerical judgments like 'There were seven sages' and certain types of relational judgment, like 'A is greater than B'.

We need not discuss logical issues at length, apart from looking at the consequences of an unqualified acceptance of the traditional formal logic.

As both Whitehead and Russell point out, the subject-predicate form of judgment is closely linked with the idea of 'substance'. Clearly there are some terms, such as 'The Empire State Building', 'Caesar' or 'I', which can function only as subjects, never as predicates in a judgment. Such can have many predicates, or different ones at different times. In that way they come to enjoy the status of entities *which change and yet stay themselves*. Thus we come to the notion of 'substance' as something that can only be the subject of a judgment, never the predicate, something that persists through change, enjoying, it seems, a special permanence.

The doctrine that all judgments can be reduced to subject-predicate form has a counterpart in the ancient idea that a thing consists of substance-plus-attributes, e.g. an apple has the attributes of roundness, solidity, etc., and when the sum of these has been written there will still appear to commonsense to remain a decided, if featureless, presence that can only be called the 'substance' of the apple.

To many, belief in a golden age is unshakeable, and it is pleasant to imagine such an age in philosophy when people believed that the world around them actually *had* those features they perceived in it, luxuriating in the conviction that the leaf was green and the fire hot because leaves were green and fires hot. If such naivete was ever the rule, it must have been shattered finally by the transmission theories of light and heat fore-shadowed in Galileo's statement above. Henceforth the heat we feel must depend, not on the presence of a splendid and terrible inhabitant of the universe, fire, but on the movements of a multitude of corpuscles in the vicinity of a 'sensitive body'.

We will imagine that I am holding out my hands to a log fire. We have in that situation a number of features: the 'moving corpuscles', the intervening air, my fingers with their nerve-endings, the complex of tendons, ganglia, etc., ending with the brain. To which of these is the heat of the fire to be attributed? It can scarcely be the corpuscles alone, or the air, or my sense-organs. Yet if we stick to the substance-attribute idea it must be an attribute of something.

The best solution seems to lie in supposing that the heat depends ultimately on the mind. This might not mean that we should say 'the mind is hot'. But we could say that the mind is conscious of heat. Thus we arrive at the idea of mind as a kind of 'signal receiving station' in contact with an external world. The signals are ideas, impressions or sense-data. Even with the receiving station it is hard to imagine what the universe outside is like, because the signals themselves give no clue; they merely glow with colour and titivate our nerve-endings and detonate noise-producing causes. All we have as guides to the outside world are certain ideas like 'substance', 'space', etc., and we are inclined to be respectful towards these because they do not glow, burn or make noises, and *ipso facto* must be more 'real'.

Another point is the necessity to distinguish between the signal—the noise or warmth-feeling—and our consciousness of it. In the end we are left with mind, i.e. 'apparent' nature, which is mental, plus 'causal' nature, i.e. those physical entities described by Galileo.

Perhaps it is not evident at first that a distinction between the world as experienced and as described by science should need a reference to mind. We might agree that a sound or colour only appears in nature when a number of conditions are fulfilled, and that these include a 'sensitive body'. Are not all such conditions physical?

This difficulty accompanies the above doctrine of substance-and-attribute. Of what is red, or hot, an attribute? To this there is no ultimate answer except 'mind'. Whitehead states the difficulty in this way: 'The reason why the bifurcation of nature is always creeping back into scientific philosophy is the extreme difficulty of exhibiting the perceived redness and warmth of the fire in one system of relations with the agitated molecules of carbon and oxygen, with the radiant energy from them, and with the various functionings of the material body. Unless we produce the all-embracing relations we are faced with a bifurcated nature.'

It is true that the instinctive division of nature into mental and non-mental, in spite of the reservation suggested above, commands a good deal of support. There is a blackout on the route of interconnection between the feeling of seeing a colour and the specified light-waves; it is necessary to elbow through this before we can talk of the waves being the 'cause' of the colour feeling. To 'see' in normal expression means to have faith in. Explanation, in scientific usage, consists in finding the general rule or pattern with which a phenomenon conforms.

'The isolation of an entity in thought,' says Whitehead, 'when we think of it as a bare "it", has no counterpart in any corresponding isolation in nature. Such isolation is merely part of the procedure of intellectual knowledge.' Paradoxically, it is still true, in a Whiteheadian sense, that even the (mistaken) feeling of isolation is a valid manifestation of 'nature itself'.

Interrelatedness is a feature of coherence, and it is chiefly against the ideal of a coherent account of nature that bifurcation offends. As Whitehead urges, it means that nearly all the world's distinctive features are contributed by mind. External reality is heatless, voiceless, a rabble of particles, and the poet should really have been praising himself when he began: *Earth hath not anything to show more fair* . . .

The criticism may be summed up in the phrase 'the fallacy of misplaced concreteness'. It is a fallacy that consists in 'presenting ourselves with simplified editions of immediate matters of fact'. The classical account rests easily in the mind. It 'works' spectacularly for material civilization, or at any rate produces devices that 'work'. Whitehead does not deny this; his point is that such must never be allowed to masquerade as an account of what we experience.

CHAPTER TWO

OCCASIONS OF EXPERIENCE

1. PRIMARY IDEAS

Whitehead's analysis of experience leads to a regrouping of various elements on organic lines. The word 'organism' suggests a living thing, and also something that is a unit amongst others. From our understanding of the concept of organism we know it to be a unit that is changing. In higher types it is a hierarchy of small-larger, humble-less humble. A man is formed of cells, which in turn are made up of molecules, which resolve themselves into atoms. Everywhere lie societies and hierarchies—in animals, plants, and even in 'inorganic' things, sticks and stones.

We think instinctively of a living organism as a unity, and when it is dead we say that the unity has been destroyed, and that is the end of it. But the most we can assume is that it has ceased to be a society of smaller organisms. Many of the cells that were identified with it go on living a dark life of their own and form new liaisons. The physical complexities of sub-molecular life continue unchecked. The smallest entities may drift and cease to be involved with one another; they do not 'die' or vanish without making enough fuss to blow up a city.

Side by side with man lie animals and the blind purposefulness of vegetation. In greater quantity lies a part of nature—we tell ourselves—where life does not enter: the inorganic world. A curious fact is the impossibility of drawing the strict categorical line between one organism and another. Nobody can say where conscious life gives way to something else. Is a dog conscious? An ant? It not, what is the difference between animal, insect and machine? It is a hard biological problem to decide when animality has become vegetative or where plants have given place to minerals. Whilst acknowledging wide differences between various states of being we are entitled to deny absolute divisions. We say as a point of observation that organic structure persists throughout nature, that while there are obvious differences in the degree of organization, it is impossible to be certain about differences in kind. But such a view, which seems on all counts reasonable, leads to the conclusion that 'organic' and 'inorganic', whilst often essential as practical distinctions, are really usurping the territory of a single class. There are simply 'organisms'.

As people and animals 'feel' and sticks and stones do not, how can the two vehicles really be one? Can the horseshoe feel the blacksmith's fire, the anvil the hammer, the flagstone the stamp of a hoof? To say otherwise sounds nonsensical. Yet when we consider the verb 'to feel' in the manner of our conclusion with 'to live', we see similarly that there is no part of nature where the presence of feeling gives way to its complete absence. 'Feeling' is nothing more than the grasping by an organism of some aspect of another, and the appropriation of this to its own nature. Such may be the action of smoked salmon on the palate, or Mozart on the ear; or in the absence of ears and palates, a mere 'concern with' or 'taking note of' or 'being affected by' other organisms.

Nothing is lost to consciousness, not even the repetitive. It would be highly speculative to say that the recipient is *exactly* the same after a feeling as before it. If such be granted to consciousness, there follows no necessity for this propensity to cease abruptly in lower beings. Animals, trees, stones—all are altered or affected by externals; all have their characteristic responses to different influences. The only just comment is that opportunities for response in simple organisms are few in the proportion of their simplicity.

Thus to understand 'feeling' in Whitehead's philosophy, the association of the dictionary word with conscious mind and 'living matter' must be given up, and the fact accepted that whilst there are differences in degree of feeling, there are no cases of its absence.

It is a pity to have to record basic ideas of Whitehead's that seem at first sight 'dotty'. The point is affected by language. In using 'feeling' in the Whiteheadian sense we are stretching a pocket handkerchief to cover a double bed. If one retains the dictionary meaning when one meets the word in Whitehead the result is bound to be unfortunate. The comedian who lurks behind the respectably inquiring part of mind pounces gladly. A world will be revealed where the salt pensively regards the sugar; the pint of beer longs to dive down a throat; the lamp post stirs in langorous anticipation with each passing dog.

Of course, Whitehead means something different when he uses the term 'feeling'. As he points out, the best exemplification is the Quaker phrase 'to have *concern* for'.

When meeting 'feeling' in Whitehead it is best to stifle all identification with sophisticated *human* feeling. Yet there is, perhaps, an analogy to be drawn. In feeling (using the word in the customary sense) we do not distinguish so clearly between subject and object as in other modes of perception. Imagine that the subject is George, a bank teller. He has a paybook thrust at him and he smites it with the date stamp and thrusts it back. The analysis of this situation would entail little to affect the 'separatedness' of (a) George, and (b) the paybook. The subject (a) is quite different from the object (b), and in spite of their split-second congruence they retain markedly separate identities.

But a new object enters the bank and swims into the field of George's perception. This is a beautiful girl with whom he falls instantly in love. The analysis of George's contract with the pay-book is here inadequate. He is still the subject (a), but the object (b) is now the girl. On that occasion it is true to say that George is not only influenced by the girl but temporarily *made what he is* by the girl's entry. If that piece of spacetime (i.e. George in the bank at 11.30 on such-and-such a date) could somehow be abstracted from the world-process and examined, George would be found to be *formed* of the object of his feeling.

'Perception' would be an adequate word to use in describing George's relation to the paybook, but misleading if used in the later instance of the girl. In that instance the only word is 'feel-ing'. In comparing the two occasions it will be in the latter that the subject is found to be partially yet unmistakably constituted of the object; and it is that situation which Whitehead has applied in generalized form throughout nature. 'Feeling' is too strong a word in our usage for such a wide generalization; but because it embraces the partial formation of the subject by the object, it is a most accurate term within Whitehead's special meaning.

'Appetition' is another Whiteheadian word. The immediate experience would not have come into being at all were it not for some appetite for potentialities as yet unrealized. Something is grasped in experience. But this is not enough. What is grasped are data—matters of fact. A datum of fact does not industriously *use* itself; it merely offers itself for use. Its use is the business of mentality in experience. The beautiful girl, sitting on a raft a thousand miles out in the Pacific Ocean, is a collection of facts that offer themselves to a mainly physical world—the raft does not fall in love, any more than the ocean or the seagulls; and the successive experiences of George, the bank teller, do not take up the facts because he knows nothing about them. When (having been rescued from the raft) she puts in her appearance at George's counter, the stage of process is set for the appetition of George's experience. The possibilities are not boundless. He could not grasp her as an arithmetical sum to be added up—she is not that sort of collection—and neither could he banish her from experience at will—she is not a mental construction. Amongst the possibilities for appetition would be a desire in George (especially if he is new to the job) to deal with her business efficiently, and in that case the grasping in George's experience of the set of facts represented by the girl would proceed to a satisfaction of a professional kind rather than falling in love.

If materialism supposes that things are pushed about by 'laws of nature', these in Whitehead's analysis are nothing but uniformities of the above kind in the feelings of the organisms that make up the universe. The consequence of a feeling is that something is changed, and if there is anything fundamental about the universe it is that everything is changing. Enduring things like the Great Pyramid are no exception. We are not aware of change when the amount available to measurement is small; it is the measuring-rod of time that is infallible in the long run.

An organism resembles a clock. We can tell the time roughly by consulting our hitherto unconscious awareness of pulses and heartbeats. Time is the measured interval between things happening, and without events or occasions of any sort there would be no time. To say that things happen 'unchanged' is to speak loosely for convenience. Violent rapidity and tortuous slowness cannot be noticed by our bodily equipment, and for such measurements we invent apparatus. Again we have the discovery of degrees only, for no difference in kind exists between what is altering in a flash and the appearance of the infinitely static. Feverish electrons and torpid mountains alike experience change.

Change arises from the concern or reaction between one thing and another which Whitehead calls 'feeling', and is everywhere. With each occasion of feeling it is true to say that the thing which has the feeling is altered. The old has made way for the new. Indeed, the new can only arise when the old has made way for it, and that is not possible until the old has gone.

If every occasion of feeling demands change, every change gives rise to *novelty*. The universe creates and re-creates itself as it goes along. Examples of imagined experience may make this clear. Tom Smith picks up a newspaper and sees a photograph with the caption, 'Patricia Jones at Monte Carlo'. He is not interested, i.e. the feeling he gets from the photograph is barely conscious. But it may reasonably be said of him, (a) that before the event he was a man who did not know that one Patricia Jones was at Monte Carlo, and (b) after the event he was aware of this fact. It would be wrong to regard him as unchanged, however small the difference between his past and present states, because some future happening might lead him to remember the photograph, and that would be impossible for the Tom Smith who existed before the experience.

Another man, Tom Jones, sees the photograph and slumps weakly into his chair. It is his wife whom he had long thought dead. He too is changed, but violently.

As a non-human example, take the ticking of a clock, or rather, one particular tick. In its humble way the clock also exhibits the introduction of novelty, and the way of the clock does not differ in kind from those of Messrs Smith and Jones. The single tick is an occasion, something has happened. Before the tick the clock had lived, say, 10,963 hours and thirty-one seconds. After the tick it has lived for the same period plus thirty-two seconds! One day the continual friction of its parts will write *finis*; it will end in the ashcan. It is a different clock after the occasion of the single tick, one that is a second nearer that fate than it was before, one that has undergone some rearrangement of its molecules as a result of the friction of the single tick.

'Organism' and 'feeling' are Whiteheadian concepts of a lesser status than one which signifies the whole character of the universe as experienced. That character is 'process'. The universe 'is' logically a process. Process means a building up and breaking down; it involves feeling, change and novelty. A picture being painted displays these qualities. (To simplify the allegory, however, it is best to imagine the molecules of paint creating their own patterns through their mutual feelings, and that the artist—God—is temporarily absent. He will be introduced later.)

Process is always producing the new and dismissing the old. A feather, shall we say, is being painted in the hat of a person in a portrait. The picture of a woman without a feather has been abolished; instead there is something new—a woman with a feather. But the past is determined—it cannot be altered—and thus the new is affected and determined by it. The hat, in its featherless past, appeared on the canvas in a certain perspective, and the feather, when it is painted, is affected by this and appears on the canvas in the correct perspective. Further, one might say that the *character* of the past must be conformed with by the present. We will imagine that the hat belongs to the portrait of an Edwardian coster queen; in consequence, when it is painted in, the feather is an ostrich feather—not the sort of feather you would expect to see, for instance, on a Tyrolean trilby.

The character of the *future* is conformed with by the present. However exuberant the creative urge, the feather is not painted so large that it ends on the back of the canvas. It is as if it is already known that the picture is to appear in a frame of a certain size. Thus the present is determined by both past and future; an event or occasion embodies both what has gone and what is to come. Everything moves with aim towards some resting-place, some satisfaction. In our allegory, the end towards which creativity struggles is a finished picture, qualified to influence, with all the authority of a fact, an unfinished future.

It is the element of novelty which, stubbornly, has persisted above or apart from the present, which qualifies the picture as a work of art. This completes the allegory, for Whitehead insists, with another stretching of a familiar word, that all feeling is essentially *aesthetic*. Occasions fail or succeed with reference to the ideal relevant to them. 'There is a rightness attained or missed, with more or less completeness of attainment or omission.'

One may see a hazard in the idea of process, i.e. the danger of giving identity to the process itself. Process has no meaning in itself, apart from what happens. You cannot say, 'There is the portrait being painted, and there is the *process* of the portrait being painted.' You can only point to the things that come out of the process. A process does not make things happen; *all that happens* is that things happen.

Here one can see the linguistic difficulty of analysing experience in terms inimical to 'simple location'. *All that happens is that things happen.* This means that the universe is made up of events or occasions—things happening—and nothing more. But things happening to *what*? Where are the things that things are happening to? The answer is that there are none, or more accurately, that none are of necessity to be involved in Whitehead's presentations. The occasions are here presented as the veritable slabs of which the universe is made. There is no substantial or enduring object to be associated anywhere with nothing happening, because the object would then itself be nothing. Even if the universe consisted of a single atom there would still be atomic events; and it would be solely because of such that the proposition 'the universe consists of a single atom' would be meaningful.

It is suggested that the exclusion of 'simply located' objects may with advantage be accepted uncritically for the time being. It is not the most difficult of Whiteheadian notions—it has features in common with much to be found in earlier philosophy —but it is forced to beat its head against the portcullis of commonsense. If it is easy to postulate occasions as the 'bricks of creation', the things to which they 'occur' die hard. However, it must be accepted, at the least provisionally, that there is no enduring stuff which events 'happen to'. There is nothing waiting to be acted on that is not itself an activity; nothing that is static. Process is the general character of everything. It is not 'making'; it is *experiencing*, which means having feelings.

To be familiar with the issues of physical science since the last century is to realize that the demand of commonsense for 'substance' is increasingly hard to satisfy. In 1900 Planck presented his theory that radiant heat is poured from its source in discontinuous bits. When I switch on an electric fire my feet are not being warmed by a continuous stream of heat but *bombarded* by tiny, separated parcels of radiant energy called *quanta*. Later, Einstein insisted that this characteristic applied to all kinds of radiant energy—light, cosmic rays, etc. This means that the common light of day is not so much streaming around me like an extensive sea; it is *bombarding* my retinae with tiny parcels of light (*photons*) having the qualities of the *quanta* postulated by Planck.

The theory that light consists of discontinuous particles seems to stand confirmed in its workaday applications, from the photo-electric cell to television. But before Planck the theory had persisted that light was *wavular*; and for certain purposes this must still be assumed. Light is *waves* or *particles* according to what scientists are observing or doing. The more nature is delved into, the farther we get from 'commonsense'; until it seems that the more inaccessible regions will have none of our ideas and display congruencies of their own in contempt of human rationality.

Between 1925 and 1928 the branch of physics called Wave Mechanics was born. The theories and experiments which gave rise to this seemed to indicate that all units of matter—protons, electrons, atoms—produced wavular patterns.

By 1930 it appeared that the universe was a system of waves (matter) plus a system of particles (radiation), the latter often themselves behaving like waves. At length a new approach allowed *quanta* to be described either as waves or particles according to the pragmatic usefulness of the situation. This later method was less concerned with the identity of separate *quanta*—a highly philosophical and theoretical pursuit—than with the mass-behaviour of matter and energy; less with the adventures of individual waves or particles as with the statistics of probability.

It may be that the statistical method will give way to something more illuminating; perhaps, instead of describing the behaviour of matter and radiation in generalized and symbolic terms, science one day will be able to return to the confident models of past ages when electricity was a fluid and the atom a hard ball. On the other hand, perhaps not. The notion of cause and effect has long been lost to a whole branch of physics; as we have noted above, the entities it pursues would be changed radically by the act of observing them. Every glance into the

D   49

subatomic world is, and perhaps must always be, through the frosted glass of uncertainty.

The evidences of quantum theory and wave mechanics, which point to finite 'slabs' of duration, may reflect Whitehead's assumption of concrete occasions. Whitehead was content to note that his analysis [is] 'perfectly consistent with the demands for discontinuity which have been urged from the side of physics'.

2. ANATOMY OF OCCASIONS

As we have seen, for the purposes of the analysis of experience, Whitehead selects the temporal occasion and presents it as one of the 'bricks' of which the universe is built. Apart from the technical refinements of Whitehead's philosophy, it is not at all hard to acknowledge as a rule-of-thumb approach that life could indeed be analysed into its separate events, each a particular piece or quantum of spacetime and each arriving at its own special unity of feeling. But Whitehead has the habit of abolishing you and us and leaving nothing but the occasion. At the moment of the occasion I am nothing but the occasion itself. The occasion is a growth of feeling and an ultimate unity, and I am that growth and that unity. My actuality, my concreteness, is to be defined by what is present in the occasion, whether derived from the past or conceptually turned towards the future, whether concerned with some present physical feeling or with an idea plucked from empty air.

This is not to say that all or any of the elements need be *conscious*, i.e. objects of that special self-awareness which seems peculiar to human beings. Many, if not most, of our transactions lack consciousness in so far as they are reflexive. In any case, consciousness seems to fade as one descends the scale of creation. Unconscious elements are never by that token unimportant. I stand at dusk in the garden and light my pipe. The flower closes its petals as the evening gathers. The world-process moves on; and who is to judge whether my action, illuminated by consciousness, is of more significance to process than the flower's?

The theory of occasions is bound to seem strange unless we can relate it to commonsense empiricism and convince ourselves that it derives from that everyday notion, an experiencing subject confronted by an object. In his early writings Whitehead starts from something akin to the commonsense account of things. From this his theory of occasions evolves. At first sight it seems complicated. But the difficulties of the 'commonsense' view of mutually independent entities are so enormous that Whitehead often appears in the clarifying rôle.

The idea of an occasion is logical. It involves the defining of an entity in terms of its relations with others and not by inimitable and unsharable qualities of its own. As a concept it is also in conformity with daily experience; for we seldom know objects *in themselves* as colours and shapes called cats, rugs, ashtrays, and nothing more. On the contrary, such things are actually felt as influencing and shaping the present occasion.

If we are to understand Whitehead it is required of us to discuss an occasion as if two distinct factors were necessary to it: the subject (the experiencing thing) and the object (the thing experienced). It would actually be more correct to say that the subject/object relation is necessary to *us* in understanding an occasion. For the occasion is more primitive and fundamental than the subject/object relation or situation. The experiencing thing, and the thing experienced, are, as it were, abstractions from the unity of an occasion. It is as if the occasion itself, the actual entity and living organism, knows nothing about them; it is as if we were *forced* to consider occasions by way of the subject/object situation because our minds are so *very* deeply scored with the assumption that the world is filled with substantial and independent objects with qualities of their own.

The speed of light is finite. Accordingly the object of an occasion must precede it in time. If I see a chair the 'seeing' is the result of light-waves having travelled from the chair to me. Therefore the perception I have of the chair is the result of something that happened *prior* to the perception.

The occasion, involving me as subject and the chair as object, may be rooted in the physical; in other words, the sight of the chair may not 'register' (as in the case of the woman and the dripping tap). But the chair may cause the occasion to have a conceptual part: 'thoughts' will arise.

The conceptual part must be regarded as contemporaneous with the occasion. It might be a feeling that I would like to sit in the chair. A bit of the spatial world has literally been 'given' to me in the form of a perception, and derives from the immediate

past. Another bit, the chair in its functional capacity, is illuminated by consciousness, or in its absence by the blind growth
of feeling. This illumination or growth is the 'present'.

The unit of being, the occasion, is the fusion of all the other
occasions which enter into it objectively—*this* chair, chair-like
feelings, memories of other chairs, etc. A feeling that I would
like to sit in the chair is a *unification* of my actual world as I am
situated in my particular piece of spacetime.

What I feel is already there, i.e. the chair. It is impossible to
alter that: the chair, as object, is completely determined. The
light-waves arrive, a message goes to my brain; the result is the
chair. The chain of cause and effect cannot be broken: I cannot
choose to see a blue chair if it is a brown one.

But how I *feel* the chair, this is not determined. In our example
I wish to sit down. I could equally choose to go on standing, to
turn the chair upside down or break it to bits with an axe. I am
free with regard to the feelings which make up my subjectivity.
It is only when I am considered as an object that I am not free.
If I have red hair I cannot avoid giving red perceptions to others.
If I step off a cliff I fall like a stone. But I can decide subjectively
to dye my hair and keep away from cliffs. To that extent I am
self-made.

Once the perception is ended it becomes a reference or datum
for future perceptions. I stop perceiving the chair, dismiss the
attendant feelings and turn to the sideboard and a new occasion.
But I am not the same person. A particular chair has been added
to whatever makes me what I am. When I turn away I have been
enriched, however trivially, by the past occasion. The chair-
feeling is no longer a living thing. It has become a 'stubborn fact'
available for inheritance. Thus I am able to learn from experience.

We noted in the first chapter certain long-standing criticisms of
cause and effect originating in Hume's *Treatise of Human Nature*.
As Professor Ayer points out, Hume was not so much attacking
our notions of causality as defining them. The important point
about his analysis of the statement 'A causes B' is the assumption
that A and B each refer to a sense-impression which is identifiable
without reference to the other, such as (a) the turning on of the
tap, (b) the gush of water. Considered in such a way, a sense-
impression offers itself to understanding in the guise of 'substance', i.e. the independent, relationless thing. This is the sort of

idea we are holding when we notice that there is no inherent connection between the turning on of the tap, or the throwing of the electrical switch, and whatever follows. It is a legacy of the dogma —on which, as we have noted, human systems of language are founded—which tells us that all relationships must finally be reducible to that of substance and quality; for if we are, indeed, stranded in a universe of independent substances, the connections between events must nowhere be apparent in anything that happens to us. In order to 'explain' the connections we must have resort to science, which bears an applicability to sense-experience too similar to mythology when it comes to the kind of explanation we are seeking.

Whitehead's occasions, on the other hand, are not independent in the above sense; they can be identified only with reference to an environment of other occasions in which, so to speak, they are embedded. When we assert a relationship between the tap and the gush of water, the situation *can then* be more than a chance juxtaposition of two elements. Since we cannot have the tap without the environment, and since that environment includes plumbing, wells, reservoirs, hands and brains, there is an element of necessity in that the gush of water follows the turning-on of the tap. There is also an *empirical* element, for before the gush 'happens' a complete stranger to our domestic civilization would know merely that the tap must be related to *some kind* of environment; it is only when the water follows that he is given the details of that environment, i.e. plumbing, reservoirs, etc.

It is clear that the strict result of a substance-quality universe is bewilderment as to how one event can be the cause of another. Whitehead's justification of induction, briefly noted in the last chapter, is in terms of the essentially interrelated pattern of process. There must be an element of uniformity throughout the universe, and this lies between the occasions of experience. The idea is followed faithfully throughout his writings, leading, as we shall see, to a disagreement with Einstein on the question of the homogeneity of spacetime.

In speaking of occasions above we have employed the sort of terms that are grammatically proper to individuals. We have illustrated the character of an occasion by describing everyday acts like that of perceiving a chair. It is proposed to return to this type of illustration, because the sphere of mental activity by human beings affords the best possible vocabulary for the clear description of what Whitehead means by occasions. It should be acknowledged at this stage, however, that Whitehead's occasions are far removed in scale from the activities of humankind, which at best provide mere parallels for apt description. The occasions as conceived are atomistic and perishing. They correspond as a concept with the pulses or minute rhythms of nature which have not only in the past suggested themselves to poetic minds but have emerged in various guises as scientific entities.

The occasion has duration and is the vehicle for something happening; nevertheless it does not change in itself. The endowment of duration removes it from the category of the geometrical points and durationless instants employed in mathematics; these are treated by Whitehead in his method of 'extensive abstraction' referred to below. It is not synonymous with what would normally be spoken of as an 'instant', because one uses the word, however loosely, to stand for the minimum piece of duration that has seen *some change*. Therefore, in common parlance, it seems correct to imagine the Whiteheadian occasion as 'less than an instant'. It would not be proper, however, to associate the idea with the term commonly used to denote, conceptually, a sudden arrest and slicing of spacetime, i.e. 'specious instant'; for although change is absent from this concept, the implication is present of a petrifying surgical operation on experience, and the term is of something durationless.

The organization of occasions into societies and nexus and the consequent freedom for organic relations is discussed below. In the meantime, for the sake of clarity, we will continue, when necessary, to use terms that are strictly appropriate to organisms of greater complexity than the single occasion.

3. FEELINGS AND PROCESS

The Whiteheadian occasions, it has been said, are experiences of feeling. In all feelings there are things felt and things which feel. The 'things felt' are the objects for the occasion, the 'things which feel' the subjects.

We have noted that feelings are not confined to consciousness but occur in sticks and stones. We have seen how, in order to understand a stone 'feeling', it is necessary to enlarge the definition by ridding the term of its connections with conscious life. Once that is done, a simple state of 'being affected' is enough. As everything is affected by everything else, 'feeling' as so defined is met with everywhere. If human beings are affected in complexity, sticks and stones are affected more simply: that is all.

'Feeling' is used by Whitehead as a broad generalization of the sort of experience that takes place when two entities connect in the object-subject relation. More complex beings get something else from that relation, i.e. knowledge. If we define 'feeling' as above, we may say that knowledge is an aspect of some type of feeling, i.e. the type that persists in memory, or in Whiteheadian language, enjoys a rich degree of inheritance from occasion to occasion. The possibility of knowledge lessens as we go down the scale. There is no chance of a cabbage or a lump of coal 'knowing' anything at all; they feel the knife or the fire without knowledge.

The Whiteheadian word 'prehension' is the more familiar 'apprehension' shorn of certain connections, e.g. with physical senses, consciousness, etc. In Whitehead the word becomes a 'grasping' by an occasion whereby it attains its own concretion.

If I am looking at a picture in a gallery it is the picture that is felt, and is the object of that occasion, and I am the feeler, the subject. It would be commonsense to regard me as the passive receiver of some influence from the picture. I stand there; I am bombarded with light from the daubed canvas, and the result in my mind, say, is an impression of the Rokeby Venus. But the idea of passive receptivity finds no place in Whitehead. The subject of the occasion (myself) is not a substantial and completed entity 'standing there' and waiting to be acted on by the picture. In some way the subject (myself) comes into being as a result of the influence of the picture, or in Whiteheadian terms, the actual entity that is the picture is 'prehended' by a concrescing entity as subject. This is definitely not the traditional way of thinking. Where and what was I before I happened to come across the picture?

The answer lies in Whitehead's account of a person as an historic route of occasions. Each is nothing more than its special feeling, and it is impossible to feel unless the datum to be felt exists. The occasions that form the historic procession are called 'myself' or 'John Smith' as a matter of symbolic reference. Each is a renewal of being; each a unitary event 'thrown up' by some object; for I am nothing apart from my life, my life is nothing apart from its experiences, and the latter are quite simply *events*. Thus in each occasion I am constituted of the object felt. Not, however, in too exclusive a sense, for 'I' am the route, and each occasion in the route is constituted of the fusion of certain past occasions into unique synthesis. The 'constituting' is the process. Thus the subject— myself confronted by the Rokeby Venus —comes on the scene *later* than the object.

If the character of things is process and the occasions distinct and separated entities, how does the route persist? What 'driving force' ensures that one event will be followed by another?

While I am looking at the Rokeby Venus I am slave to the precise intention of process, i.e. the production of subjective feeling. But the feeling does not last for ever. It attains what Whitehead calls its 'satisfaction' when a point is reached which is described as unity of feeling. Clearly there can be no *completed* feeling that is not a unity. To take the 'specious instant' as an example, my identity is not the arms, legs, cells and atoms postulated by science so much as my feeling in that instant. The feeling may be complex in the sense that its *object* may be complex (its object could well be the universe) but in no sense might it be said to be more than one feeling. As soon as this oneness is achieved, the occasion, with its subjective unity and concrete reality, is over. It has gone and can never live again.

The departure from the familiar is obvious. In everyday terms the 'concrete reality' is external to my feeling and resides in the 'substances' represented in our example by my mind and the Rokeby Venus respectively. In this view my subjective responses to the picture are literally neither here nor there. They *may* affect my body in some completely inexplicable fashion, or my persona, id, soul or whatever else may be postulated. Or they may have no effect upon anything.

By taking experience as the reality Whitehead acquires the paving-stones of process. For the successor to a particular experience takes that experience as object. Apart from the inevitable element of novelty, the subjective pattern is repeated. More simply, my perception of the Rokeby Venus, having evolved into a unity of feeling, falls from the status of subjectivity and becomes a fact. I am then drawn as an element into the constitution of some other occasion. This could be one in which I experience myself subjectively as a society of facts in which my recent experience with the Rokeby Venus is numbered. As long as I have any knowledge of the Rokeby Venus I am that society. Thus the perished subjective experience lives on as object. It enjoys what Whitehead calls 'an objective immortality'.

There are two features of process to be noted above, i.e. the 'concrescence' with which my feeling grows and becomes a unity, and the 'transition' of that unity into an objective matter of fact. These words of Whitehead's are the equivalent of anatomical terms; he is seeing the occasions as veritable corpuscular organisms, organisms extended in time as well as space and incorporating ideas as well as physical features.

Although, as proposed above, human terms are to be employed for the sake of clarity, the employment of a man in an art gallery as an illustration is a drastic, even a misleading, simplification. What has happened is not a mere contact between myself —one thing—and the Rokeby Venus—another. Both myself and the painting are centres of monumental complexity; and that complexity, all that can be summed up in the ideas of a human being and a treasured painting like the Rokeby Venus, is present in the occasion.

Individual worlds are never alike. Imagine two patrons of the gallery to be present: Tom and Dick. They are both contemplating the Rokeby Venus and not having the same experience. Tom's inheritance of the past has not been Dick's. It may be that the feeling thrown up in Tom's case is the categorical reverse of Dick's. Tom's actual world in that occasion is made of all the objects—past, present, even in a sense future—which enter into it. Whenever someone is professing to talk or write about the actual world he is dealing either with physical feelings experienced in the past, or ideas apprehended in the present, or with both. The world is always relative to some occasion of experience, never to a 'thing' standing somewhere out on its own.

If we ignore the relativity and postulate the 'thing' the result is satisfactory for all purposes except philosophy. We may 'feel' the world as apparently extended and populated with things and thereby participate in actual occasions which become objective matters of fact. *Truth* has no effect, in Whitehead's view, on the concrescence of an occasion. If the world is felt to be a mechanism with material parts, that is still a feeling, and the 'mistake'—if such it be—is drawn into the objective make-up of the universe. Possibly there are still people who think of the earth as flat. That they do so is a 'stubborn fact', equally a part of reality as the arguments which prove the earth to be round.

An occasion is a unique being, firmly fixed in reality. It is misleading to imagine that it stands in a relation with the universe in the sense of the universe being some kind of framework outside it. If the framework exists at all in a concrete sense it can be no more than the potentialities exhibited by the sum-total of occasions. Thus, when we talk of the universe apart from the occasions, we are envisaging something of a lesser actuality, something that is what it is because of what happens. The 'framework'—spacetime—does not influence the occasions. It is the other way round. There is really no need for a person to feel tiny and insignificant in comparison with some astronomer's inter-galactic mileages; the kitten playing on the carpet is more important.

Many objects enter into an occasion and cause feelings to grow and participate in the final unity. These are 'there'; they are 'stubborn facts'; they cannot be altered at will any more than that someone could turn a tree into a lamp post by looking at it. These objects are largely reproduced in the resulting feeling.

A way of describing the feeling one has of a cow is a 'cow-like' feeling, or of the scale of A Major, 'a musical feeling in A Major'. But if this were the whole story there would be no creative advance in the world, and process would consist of finite occasions infinitely repeated. We know the reverse to be the truth; there is novelty and there is growth.

It is the feeling partner in an occasion—the subject—which decides how the diverse elements thrown up by experience are finally to be felt. This decision Whitehead calls the 'subjective aim' of an occasion. I wish to know or feel the world in a certain way, and the elements available as objects of feeling are turned that way by my subjective aim. They are organized, repressed or emphasized, as the case may be, in accordance with the needs of the final unity. That is, they are governed from the future. But the final satisfaction, the unity, is not determined in advance as the elements of a mechanical universe would necessarily have to be determined. It is the creative factor, the world-canvas for-ever painting itself.

But if the occasion is truly finite and unique, why is it that things seem to persist through change?

Every occasion affects its successors. Whatever follows my experience with the Rokeby Venus has to include that experience as an inescapable fact. The successor is not already 'there' to be conditioned passively by my previous experience, but is thrown up by, or emerges from, that experience. To some extent it is bound to reproduce something of the previous experience. I am changed by my contact with the Rokeby Venus, and it is myself as changed that must enter the next occasion as object. I carry my historic past with me. Thus the world seems to persist through change.

When we take an object, such as an apple, and ask ourselves why it is round, coloured, hard—why it has apple-like qualities—there are two possible answers. We may say that it has the qualities because it has become like that: or that it has become like that because it is an apple. The first answer, of course, is in terms of mechanism, or causation, and the second in terms of teleology.

In using the mechanical explanation we imply that every event is determined by another that has preceded it. In the teleological explanation we do not necessarily drop the idea that events are determined, but we say that they are determined by what lies ahead, not what has gone before. In the case of the apple we take its completed growth and final identity as the causal factor in all the events that followed the germinating of the seed. It does not grow *because* the seed germinated; it grows because, being what it is, it must strive to attain complete applehood.

This principle fits Whitehead's idea of nature as a process of 'becoming', with the proviso that an element of novelty or pure creativity must invariably be present in each occasion. But although in the classical teleological theory the end was some-thing fixed, determining the thing's growth towards it, White-head would insist that the end is really present in the thing (i.e. the occasion) itself, just as the end of a race may be said to be present in the running of it, in so far as the competitors and spectators are envisaging nothing else.

In no uncertain sense it is easy to accept that the past is represented by the present. It is true that *past is past* and cannot be repeated; it is also true that the present would not be what it is if it were not for the past.

But it is not easy to see how the *future* can be represented by the present. The past, after all, existed once as a living occasion; the future has not yet existed; the present alone exists. How can non-existence have any influence on anything? Before we answer, it must be decided whether 'non-existence' is the right expression to use for something that is 'not yet'. It seems obvious that the first letter to be opened by the Pope on New Year's Day in the year 2200 does not now exist. But it is not so obvious that the first letter to be opened *in a week's time* does not exist. Further, it is almost a falsehood to deny existence to events even closer at hand—say, the present sentence as a completed whole. At the position in time when I wrote the words 'say the present', the words 'sentence as a completed whole' lay in the future. But they were represented in a perfectly real and forthright manner in the present. Their sense had already been determined by the past, i.e. the beginning of the sentence, and the future was under compulsion to conform. True, the compulsion is far from a rigid sort. I might have written '*paragraph* as a completed whole' or '*phrase . . .* '; or I might have had a fatal seizure after writing the word 'present', in which case the sentence, paragraph or phrase would never have been completed. It is enough that the *occasion* in which I wrote the word 'present' is followed by another which assimilates the objective data, whether the datum is an incomplete sentence or an incipient seizure.

Therefore the future is stamped indelibly with the hallmark of the present, but the marks fade as more distant futures are considered. I can foretell the events of the next second with small chance of error, but I can only guess wildly at the next hundred years.

However, instead of a specious present or hypothetical point in time, we must recollect that we are considering Whitehead's occasion with its finite 'slab' of duration. We know that it is 'thrown up' by what happened in the past. But it ends as an influence upon something that is to happen in the future. It has in itself the relationships it is to have with the future, and carries the necessities to which the future will have to conform.

So far we have taken little notice of novelty. Whitehead, we know, insists on a residue of novelty in each occasion. If the future were wholly caused by the present nothing new could happen. The repetitive tendency is precisely why we regard stones and suchlike things as exceptionally 'dead' and 'enduring'. The residue of novelty in the route of occasions called a stone, as we have already seen, has been so small that it may almost be said that the present has repeated the past. Only *almost*—for stones weather; mountains grind the minerals inside them into change. Novelty is real and universal; the present decides how the past should be felt, and the result is new data for the future. The fact that one thing is affected by another is enough for us to affirm the presence of novelty. Repetition alone would mean a world of stasis, and there is no evidence that static objects can exist anywhere. The kind of change involved in the crumbling of mountains is of a lowly and familiar order. The novelty here is almost confined to the fact that it is *this* mountain which is crumbling in *that* way. Higher in the scale we see the novelty that means more to humankind; the occasions, as effects from the past and causes for the future, throw up *Hamlet*, the Rokeby Venus or the Ninth Symphony.

If past and future are to have relations with the present there must be a causal connection between them. But what about relations between different occasions in the present?

It is clear that there can be no direct causal connection between such occasions. As pointed out above, the subjective feeling arising, say, out of my inspecting the Rokeby Venus comes on to the scene *later in time* than the object. A person standing by my side may have a similar sort of feeling, also derived from the object. But it is obvious that there is no causal chain between my private perception and his. This means that the first letter to be opened by the Pope on New Year's Day, 2200, is not linked with my experience at this moment unless my experience can determine it causally. Past and future do not exist in the sense of anything amorphous and absolute, but as strands of cause-and-effect in complicated interconnection. Perhaps 'texture' is the best analogy. It is as if a tremendous tapestry of intricate design were being woven. The stitches conform to the idea of what a stitch should be—the thread retains its identity as such from stitch to stitch. But the weaver creates the pattern as he goes along. The weaver is monstrous like an Indian god. He has countless hands, each engaged simultaneously on the tapestry. Each hand has to do with a particular strand or lineal process of stitches. In that way the contemporary stitches in different strands enjoy a freedom from mutual causal connection.

It is plain, however, that contemporary occasions must enjoy *some* interconnection, if only because of the conformity that is so noticeable between them. All over our tapestry stitches are stitches and thread is thread. Even if no pair of stitches at a given instant are exactly alike, there is still something predominately 'stitchlike' about them. This conformity is secured by their common past and future. As far as I know, there is no causal connection between myself and the Pope at this moment, but we both spring from a common stock which extends back into the past and reaches into the future. We might well display marked differences, but these are seen to be superficial when it is acknowledged that we are each recognizable instantly as members of the human race.

CHAPTER THREE

ORGANIC RELATIONS

---

1. GROUPS OF OCCASIONS

The task of expounding Whitehead's philosophy might be said to be easier where the larger groupings of his actual entities are involved. At least it is possible to draw examples with greater fidelity from the macroscopic world of man-sized organisms.

The character of an organic structure is one that involves the participation of parts in wholes and of wholes in parts. The different parts of our bodies are mutually dependent, and they also determine one another. This is noticeable in varying degrees. The loss of a leg leads to a drastic lapse in the organic structure of the limb itself, but a lapse far less drastic in the trunk that is left. The limb 'dies', which is the same as saying that it reverts to a less elaborate type of organization. The body readjusts itself, acquires new and compensatory skills and remains an organism of apparently the same status as before. On the other hand, the removal of our *heads* would disrupt the whole organism! It is the difference between blowing up the city hall and destroying the national seat of government.

To understand the relations and organizations of occasions whereby they are built up into the complexities with which we have to do, one has to consider two main characteristics of the former: (a) conformity with past and future, (b) order.

The way in which both past and future somehow participate in the present has been discussed. It is with order that we are now concerned.

With some difficulty it is possible to ignore the tug of past and future, to drop all one 'knows' and experience the succession of events neutrally as they are given. This 'givenness', as a quality of the world, is met in states between sleeping and waking or on regaining consciousness after an accident. Nearly everyone has lived through the disturbing moment when all historical sense is lost. One has awakened, perhaps, from an unusually deep sleep; for a time one merely gapes at shapes in their pristine immediacy. Then the perceptual paraphernalia of the world recurs with a rush; the past floods the room; symbolic labels—'chair', 'carpet', 'dressing table'—take the place of the stark and rather terrifying 'givenness'.

If such a neutrally receptive state could be analysed it seems certain that the succession of events would be found to display neither order nor disorder. All that could be said of them would be that they displayed raw presence. Whatever it is that lends a sense of order or disorder must be something other than the 'givenness'. Is it perhaps the purposiveness of a journey towards an end as conceived in the teleological principle? Do our notions of order or disorder derive, not from the past, but from the future?

Broadly, contrasts tend to promote unity, incompatibles to disrupt. Contrasts form patterns: incompatibles tend to break up the patterns. We have seen that there is only one end to an occasion, i.e. unity of feeling. There is not, however, one end or grand event towards which all occasions move, but a multiplicity of ends, each appropriate to a special grade of occasions. The organization of occasions tends to express the ideal of limited ends; the dog is always striving to be more doglike, the tree more treelike, than before. This is more of an Aristotelean than a Whiteheadian statement; Whitehead would say that the occasion is self-creative, and that this activity aims at the unification of all its contributory elements. The quality of the unity of feeling in successive occasions reaches intensity in the 'maturity' of an organism. After that the rhythm lessens, the patterns break up, the incompatibles creep in.

Degree of feeling and intensity of maturity depend, therefore, on the order or disorder of the objective data. Clearly, if large things like trees or men are to be spoken of as displaying order, we must look for explanation to a particularly orderly relation between the occasions. But it is precisely *because* this is orderly that the tree or man exist at all! The Whiteheadian word for tree or man is 'society'. Like most of his words, this has no such simple application as 'Here comes a society called James.' A society is a group of occasions which endure in a special sense. The enduring factor owes itself to their common form. All the members of a society show similarities which are inherited from occasion to occasion.

The definition of a society is not confined to things extended in space like trees and men. The life of a tree or a man may be thought of as an historic route of occasions in the course of which innumerable societies are born and perish, existing together in every kind of relation. If we learn a language, for instance, the group of occasions dating from the learning of the language to the loss of that learning will be a society in the Whiteheadian sense. The myriad members of this society will have a common form for inheritance, i.e. knowledge of the language.

For reasons suggested earlier, there cannot, in spite of the clamour of commonsense, be a society of *contemporary* occasions.

All completed societies lie in the past. All living societies are incomplete, because new members are constantly being added. No societies, living or dead, are to be thought of as existing in isolation. Apart from the internal constitution which holds a society together, there is always a necessary dependence on other societies. These 'others' are known scientifically as the environment. Take a man and place him in isolation, e.g. in a vacuum subject to no influences, and he would vanish like a spark or boojum. But, of course, there are no places free from influences; the most that could be done would be to transform him into a more simple society. Man needs air, food, certain gravitational circumstances, pressures and temperatures. The idea of any-thing apart from its environment is an abstraction.

Whitehead refers to the universe as a 'seamless coat'; which rather tempts one to believe that he is a monist. The coat, how-ever, has a pluralistic structure. Definiteness resides in things less general than the universe as a whole. When we use the word 'identity' in connection with a society we are pointing to a characteristic of the separate occasions in time whereby they conform with each other by inheritance. Such a line of occasions is an enduring object. Strictly, an enduring object *has* no identity in the familiar usage, but only in the sense by which we understand a *defining character*—e.g. we call the living group a man, 'Mr Smith' *because* it endures. This is not the same as crediting a man with absolute identity. The only things with absolute identity are the occasions, which are atomistic and perishing. There is a Whiteheadian flavour in Mr Nigel Denis's extraordinary novel *Cards of Identity* which makes this point.

Every society must have a background of which it is a part. Thus the familiar idea of a society—the British, the French, the Royal Academy, etc.—is also a society in the Whiteheadian sense. The universe is a hierarchy of such. At the top they display a high degree of generality—the biological class of mammals, for example. At the bottom all is narrow specialization, e.g. an atom of hydrogen. All have their own internal, as well as external, conditions; it is on the fulfilment of these that their 'identity' depends. Although I am one particular man, I live in the environment of a nation, and I must observe certain national laws or the environment will punish me. Further, I must live in the environment of animal nature or die for lack of food and sleep. Again, I must observe the rules of the environment of material bodies, and keep away from precipices, high temperatures and extremes of pressure.

There is an obvious difference, however, between the society we mean when we speak of a man and the kind intended by 'the French' or 'the Royal Academy'. If anything happens to a single member of the Royal Academy there follows no *necessary* effect on the society; the Royal Academy may not need to know anything about it. But if something happens to a single member of the society called 'a man' there is far more likelihood of a direct effect upon the whole. This is because the latter types of society enjoy what Whitehead calls 'personal order'. The members can be ordered serially in time in accordance with the process of inheritance from one occasion to the next. This is not true of the Royal Academy, although it contains many sub-societies which have personal order. Thus we can never 'see' the Royal Academy; we can only see the enduring objects, the men, paintings, buildings and bits of paper, which belong to it.

The notion of personal order is grounded in commonsense. Considered singly, Whitehead's occasions are unitary 'bricks' and to that extent lack organization; but together or in groups they form systems. Thus the occasion called an electron is some-

66

thing remote and primitive; fused into a hydrogen atom it begins
to show character; conscripted into a raindrop it seems suddenly
to make sense. Such a group of occasions does in fact appear to
us as a kind of order; in our everyday transactions we would
stop calling it 'occasions' and think of it as 'thing'. Each thing
—raindrop, lump of quartz, or even a human being called Miss
A—displays *structure*. It consists of successive strata of groups,
each showing a new kind of order which shares the general
order of the whole; an order which in turn is seen to be nothing
but another orderly grouping within some larger system; until
we arrive at the idea of totality, the universe.

Let us look at the mutual relations of such groups by taking
three sets of occasions; first, say, a set called *a bacterium in the
large intestine of Miss A*, secondly another set known as *the
digestive system of Miss A*, and thirdly the group of occasions
which are collected under the symbol *Miss A*. Each of these
groups, with its internal condition of orderliness, can be thought
about as existing in several ways. First, from the viewpoint of
the relations with each other of its parts. Secondly, from the
aspect of an external observer whom it affects as a unity. Thirdly,
from the point of view of an occasion within the group. From
this third viewpoint the unity of the group may be experienced,
even though the observer happens to belong to it. Thus Miss A
is aware of the historic and internally ordered procession of
occasions called *Miss A*, and also of occasions within the group
(her stomach troubles) and of events outside (town, country,
planet, cosmos). But whether she thinks of herself as a closed
system or as a cog in some larger mechanism, one fact emerges.
She is not simply a 'subject' in contact with the 'objects' of the
world, but a local concentration of being, barely distinguishable,
were it not for the extreme emphasis of personality, from the
greater mass making up the universe. It is inaccurate, for
instance, to talk of values being 'in' her but not 'in' the universe.
One might as glibly speak of Orlando being 'in' *As You Like It*
but not 'in' Shakespeare's works.

There is an obvious difference between enduring objects
themselves, e.g. the difference between Miss A and a lump of
quartz. These both enjoy personal order, but there is something
else of importance which the one has predominately but not
the other. This something is consciousness, somewhat a large

subject. Whitehead disappoints many readers by his habit of minimizing the importance of consciousness. It is almost as if he dislikes humanists! That such a judgment would be superficial is apparent from the work of his life as a whole, rather than from this single element of his philosophy. In fact, from the 'playing down' of consciousness the rest of the universe derives a majesty which, one feels, might not otherwise be its due. Whitehead is a refreshing change from Bergsonian metaphysics and the humanism of the first decade of the present century. It is to Whitehead's view of specifically human attributes that we now turn.

2. LIFE: MIND: CONSCIOUSNESS

Man, in Whitehead, is just another society of occasions, like ships, shoes or sealing wax. As we have noted above, he refuses to give man an exalted place. He would admit, doubtless, that man's feelings are organically more interesting than those of a fish, but analytically there is nothing to choose between them. Both men and fish are made up of relations with world-process. The fact that a man can write *Hamlet* and the fish do little but swim in circles is not particularly striking; far more important is the fact that both activities are born of feeling.

This apparent 'down-grading' of consciousness has distinct advantages for the understanding of nature. In fact, Whitehead has not banished mind or consciousness to the outhouse or backyard of existence; he has placed it with its fellows in the context of the real entities which make up the universe. It is still possible to say that human intellect is the vehicle of an adventure that will 'find its grave in an unimaginable future'. Meanwhile Whitehead avoids yielding unique primacy to consciousness. Man is not the monarch of all he surveys, but a particular piece of organization amongst many.

Here, as in other respects, Whitehead's analysis of experience succeeds in throwing some light on problems of mind which engaged earlier philosophers.

Rene Descartes is often called the first 'modern' philosopher. He was one of the earliest of major status to take into account the activities of science, in a contemporary sense. To him the bodies of men and animals were automata. Animals had neither feelings nor consciousness; but to the machine that comprised the body of a man was to be added the organ called 'soul'. This was said to reside in the pineal gland, where it came into contact with 'vital spirits' which ensured interaction between mind and body.

The difficulties of this theory were those of physical law itself. If the quantity of motion in the universe is constant it is clear that it cannot be increased by 'mind'. Nevertheless, said Descartes, mind can vary the *direction* of motion and thus influence the physical body.

Later it was discovered that the quantity of motion is also constant in any given *direction*, a circumstance that seemed to put paid to the Cartesian account. For the laws of dynamics were found sufficient in themselves to explain the movements of all material bodies, including those of human beings. Yet, observedly, man had a mind, and if he used his mind to decide to raise his index finger, the finger was duly raised, for all the world as if mind, and not body, controlled it. The exclusively mental and the exclusively material were daily seen to inter-act, in spite of the logical impossibility of such a thing happening.

A theory of parallelism was advanced to meet this. Both mental and physical worlds, it was said, were controlled by God and were mutually exclusive. But God had 'wound up' and synchronized them as if they were a pair of clocks. Hence-forth whatever happened in the mental world was followed faithfully by the appropriate event on the physical plane. If I willed to raise my finger, I raised it. But the one event was not the cause of the other; it was merely an appearance of causality imposed because of the perfect synchronization of God's twin kingdoms. It followed that both the mental and the physical must be absolutely determined, for the mind could not faithfully parallel the body without sharing the determinate nature of the latter. Such was the problem left for later philosophers, who wished to re-establish mind both as an influence on the physical world and as a vehicle for free will. Whitehead, as we know, generalized the concept of mind throughout nature by postulating a mental as well as physical pole in every actuality.

We have seen that there is no difference *in kind* between the life of a man and that of a stone. We have also seen that *novelty* is part and parcel of the final unity of feeling in every occasion. But the degree of novelty varies spectacularly. A growing baby is changing in great leaps. A stone also is changing, but the novel element is too small to be perceived. Instead we see its 'lifelessness'. Whilst the baby's changes are measureable daily, the stone's need the measuring-rod of geological time. Thus what we mean by 'life' is the state of a society in which the novel element is so large that it is immediately obvious. In fact, Whitehead's 'novelty', like Henri Bergson's, involves not only change but unpredictability.

In other words, life exists where mentality predominates. The highest novelty accompanies the possession of a mind, and little can be found in things that are predominately 'physical'. It is possible with some accuracy to account for the physical solely in terms of cause-and-effect, but it is not so easy to treat of mental events in the same way.

There is a not inconsiderable part of every occasion which simply repeats what has gone before. If there were not a large residue of repetition in change, we should all be lost in unfamiliar worlds with each second that passes.

In describing the above, and also the varying part that adds something new to the inevitable repetition of the past, Whitehead uses the expression, introduced above, 'a physical and a mental pole'. Subjective consciousness often makes us aware of the sharp division between these. We can only *infer* the possession of consciousness by others, and therefore an effect which other people have on our minds is one in which the physical side seems to predominate. A person might conclude himself to be the unique and single survivor of a conscious species, and that his so-called fellows were really robots, conspiring together to keep him in ignorance of the truth. Such a person would undoubtedly be no stranger to mental hospitals. In point of fact, no variety of proof could possibly be advanced with a logical necessity sufficient to rid such an unfortunate of the delusion.

Life is supposed to provide co-ordination between the parts of my body, and is called variously by writers a 'spark', 'vital principle', etc. These names are apposite, because they do not imply that *all* parts of an organism are 'alive'. In fact, most parts of people and animals are 'dead' as the term is commonly understood. The parts of me that are 'alive' are those aspects of my experience that consist of novelty, that do not merely repeat the past. These 'living occasions', being only aspects of predominately 'dead' occasions, cannot exist in their own right. There is no such thing as a society of living occasions, devoid of any subservient 'inorganic' societies. The essence of a society is inheritance. Life is not inherited; it is the novel addition, within each occasion, to whatever *is* inherited.

If there are no vital spirits of a Cartesian kind, and no 'life' in the body apart from the lives of its separate occasions, how is one to account for consciousness?—how for co-ordination?

The majority of our body-cells seem to enter successive occasions with no consciousness and little in the way of co-ordination. The cells of my pancreas or uvula appear to live their own lives; as far as my consciousness is concerned I have to read books or listen to lectures before I know that I 'have' them. True, I am persuaded that they are co-ordinated function-ally with the larger society comprising my body, but to a degree even less marked than the co-ordination of my body with groupings—nation, species, spacetime continuum—which exist outside it. Certain cells, however, enjoy a peculiar richness of inheritance with a marked endowment of novelty. These are in the brain. Now this part, and now that, says Whitehead, enjoys this richness; and thus there is produced the presiding personality at the moment in the body. There always *is* a presiding personality because of the inheritance from occasion to occasion. It follows that this personality must be an 'enduring object' in the sense already discussed.

The ways in which occasions arise out of the objective world and evolve to their final unity are many. Some are simple adversions or aversions; others are complex, e.g. evaluation, emotion, forms of consciousness. Consciousness, as Whitehead so astringently insists, is not the most important amongst the forms in which the world can be felt; it is merely different from the others in that it is not primarily appetitive. We have discussed Whitehead's use of this word. By 'appetitive' is meant the kind of feeling which urges that some possibility should be grasped in order to make a new actuality, or as better put by Whitehead, 'an urge towards the future based on an appetite in the present'.

Consciousness is a mere handmaiden to appetitive feelings. It enables such activities to be abstracted and theorized over: it is applauder and critic.

One is tempted to credit conscious entities with a monopoly of 'conceptual' feelings. This is not, of course, Whitehead's way. All entities, he insists, whether simple occasions or giant societies, have a mental side, manifested in growth, decay and change of all kinds.

Consciousness is possible without any awareness of the first-person or self as such, and only a small class of entities having *self-consciousness*, are able to say *Cogito ergo sum*.

Whitehead's 'down-grading' of consciousness is one way of pointing out that those things which may appear especially striking and important, from the point of view of self-awareness *vis-à-vis* an apprehended universe, may be elements of super-ficiality to experience as a whole. For Whitehead, consciousness analyses bits of the universe. Clearly this is a rare activity. The experience of non-human entities throughout the universe is not cognitive. Only *human* experience is of this nature, and a small amount even of that. Whitehead sees the major role of consciousness in the active savouring of whatever might be, as opposed to what *is*. From the feeling of 'might be' arise the possibilities for the imagination.

We have seen that the Cartesian problem lay in the apparent incompatability of matter and mind. These twin dominions may more conveniently be called 'mechanism and life'. Thus, freed from associations with physics and psychology, they appear the more readily as the twin aspects of a single process. In no occasion is either completely absent. The function of mechanism is the re-enlistment of the past, and each occasion displays that function. But there is also the reference to new possibilities in the environment. It is this 'clutching at novelty' that is all we can possibly mean by 'life'.

The universe contains a vast number of simple physical feelings which are 'about' other physical feelings objectivized. Such elementary occasions are apparent to us, in aggregate, as cause-and-effect. The familiar causal patterns around us are the public aspects of such feelings. When we speak of causes we refer to the objectified initial data of simple physical feelings; when we speak of effects we mean the subjective unification of feeling that emerges from the causes. These may be as big as the explosion of a volcano or too small to be noticed, such as the enduring being of a stone—a lineal series of temporal occasions 'one after another', the latest of which feels its predecessor physically and repeats it.

So much for the simple feelings. When an occasion has a 'nexus' of other actualities as its initial data, Whitehead calls the resulting unity a 'transmuted feeling'. A nexus is a group of occasions which enjoys some mutual inherent relation of a special kind. The group can be both temporal and spatial, e.g. 'all the red-haired schoolboys alive or dead'; or else predominately spatial, as 'every red-haired schoolboy now existing', or more especially temporal, such as 'the red-haired schoolboys of the past'. We have already discussed the Whiteheadian notion of a society. A society is an example of a nexus which enjoys the special character of social order.

Transmuted feelings are more advanced types of physical feeling, and their inclusion is important. The transmuted feeling is the device by which nature permits us to experience the many as one.

Consider diversity and proliferation. We know that the most minute object consists of strata and substrata of entities. Every experience we have of 'one' is really an experience of many. Therefore an idealization of the many must be involved. It is a possibility inherent in all diverse groups that they may be felt as one, and when we have the feeling of the one, when what is presented is really the many, we are not so much sampling the concrete world as actualizing one of its possibilities. We would collapse in bewilderment if the only way we could experience a meadow was by savouring individually a billion blades of grass.

Thus feelings for the many become feelings of the one. Each grain of sand is a location of simple physical feelings. Each has its own route by which its successive temporal occasions create and re-create it as an enduring object. The contemporary grains are causally independent of each other. Objective feelings are generated by each grain and enter the subjective experience of another entity—myself. But the feelings are substantially alike, and this is intolerable; so the conceptual side of my feeling takes charge and hastens to entertain the whole lot as a unity. The 'sand' idea, which in a physical sense is applicable only to each separate grain, is drawn into my experience as a whole. As we cannot probe the heart of matter, human beings are aware of no feelings that are not either (a) transmuted physical feelings, or (b) conceptual feelings.

A transmuted feeling requires mentality. Whitehead accordingly rejects the view that mind and body cannot interact. While the body is regarded as a rigid, machine-like thing, and the mind an infinitely rarified 'gas' inside it, the difficulty of interaction is insoluble. But when the occasion of experience is taken to be the concrete entity instead of the pieces of matter required by classical science and philosophy, it is obvious that mind and body are inseparables.

In experience many entities are felt as unities. But such can almost be called arbitrary abstractions from the seamless coat of existence. We see a forest, a tree, a branch, a twig, a leaf, according to whatever is the datum of the transmuted feeling; but the datum is not felt for what it is unless qualified by the appropriate idea.

3. 'ETERNAL OBJECTS'

Whitehead's philosophy contains much that is reminiscent of the classical doctrine of Universals as advanced by Plato and Aristotle. Before we can understand the relations enjoyed by the mental pole of an actual entity, it is necessary to be clear about the universal form as encountered in classical philosophy, and how Whitehead's own version of the doctrine differs from the ancient position. The nature of the Universal, as described by Plato, is well known; but at the risk of boring the reader, it is worth restating briefly, in order that Whitehead's position may be the more accessible.

The characters or qualities of things—wetness, dryness, and most other words ending in 'ness'—appear in experience under two modes. One is the particular instance, the other the universal sense. Commonsense might say that 'straightness', for instance, is known solely through the isolated cases when we meet particular straight things—this ruler and that ruler, telegraph poles, pine trees and furrows, as they occur in the landscape, example upon example. But has the idea of straightness itself no reality except in the instances of contact with straight things? Or, in some fashion, does a universal and unparticularized straightness exist somewhere? If so, what sort of existence should be allowed for this straightness? Could it possibly be as definite as the particular straight thing? Can it reasonably be said to be a mode of existence at all?

Some would reply by defining straightness as an idea and nothing more, meaning that although the qualities of things are unique to themselves—the glitter of a diamond belonging to one individual diamond and not in any sense to diamonds in general—similarities which nevertheless *do* occur between qualities give us ideas of them collectively without reference to individual things. Thus, although 'glitter' has a definite meaning, there is no mode, apart from particular glittering things, under which it may be held to exist. It is the uniformity of glittering things that gives us ideas of glitter, and beyond the instances there is nothing except the ideas. Now many do not admit that ideas can be called real until they are transformed by being 'put into practice', e.g. an idea of red is in itself nothing, but if I go and paint a sign for the Red Cross, *that* is something. Therefore an unparticularized idea of quality is a mere notion inspired by similarities, and it follows that these must be coincidences.

Thus we should look for a coincidence every time we see anything. There is a certain shape, and from our past experience, with which by coincidence the present happens to conform, we infer a table. Resemblances between the most favoured ways of looking at objects lead to the acceptance of certain aspects as 'true' or 'real'. A coin is 'really' circular, although when seen on edge it is linear.

In spite of this arbitrary aspect of qualities, the identification and enjoyment of shape, colour and all form is delightfully easy. In the case of a flagpole, any lingering doubts about its straightness could be removed by the use of a plumb. The similarity between pole and plumb 'proves' the straightness. But presumably only for purposes that are strictly human. If the pole were stuck in a lake, an intelligent fish might be justified in taking a wavy, mobile shape as the 'true' one. A microbe of submolecular size might see the pole as an expanse of shapeless motion. Even if wavy lines and shapeless motion were clearly the dominant characters for all observers, the fact would remain, according to this view, that qualities are meaningless if considered in isolation. The importance of this is near the bone of humanity when it is recalled that lives have been sacrificed for qualities called 'honour', 'freedom', etc. Can all this heroism have been wasted?

For the opposite view one looks to Plato and the mediaeval Realists. To return to the 'straight' flagpole, here it would be held that 'straightness' is an ingredient of the world, or to use a better metaphor, a mould, matrix or *form*, to which our particular flagpole struggles to approximate. It is the *being aware of the form*, and not the comparison of the flagpole with others, that makes people accept it as a straight pole; otherwise they could have no knowledge of the quality of straightness at all. A particular object like the flagpole can never be understood, or even experienced, in its individual self. It is the universal quality of straightness which makes it a reality for experience. Cancel its qualities and it is by no means certain that anything tangible remains. But in that case, what is an object? Nothing but an attempt by the physical world to exemplify some group of ageless ingredients of the spiritual world known as *The Forms*.

From the above assumption that universal forms or characters exist, to which the particulars struggle to approximate, it follows that the universal character of Goodness must itself be one of the forms. To this character the particular and imperfect acts of Smith, Jones and Robinson struggle to approximate. Smith, in giving a donation to charity, is illustrating the goodness of Smith. But it is to be assumed that Goodness exists without Smith, without anyone.

The whiteness of this piece of paper may be the same as that of the bathroom wall. The two things have nothing in common except the whiteness. In the platonic sense, whiteness is more real than white, circularity more real than a circle, goodness more real than a good man. In a word, ideas are more important than things. There is even some doubt as to the utility of *things* when it comes to practical knowledge. A painting may please one but not another; a performance that delights teenagers may seem undignified to elderly ladies. There is nothing absolute about the objects which act on our senses; everyone passes conflicting judgments about them. If they are to be known at all it is only imperfectly by speculation and opinion. One can claim neither moral, aesthetic nor scientific knowledge of mere sensations.

We can, and do, claim knowledge, but the reason is that mere sensations, removed altogether from universal characters, are scarcely ever experienced. In the platonic sense, the expression 'knowledge of things' is idiomatic; what is meant would be accurately expressed as knowledge of universals—of the world of forms. The form alone is real. The groping towards it revealed in the particular instance is only imperfectly real. Announcements about a spot being red are opinions; a colour-blind person might decide that the spot is grey. The *form* of redness is the real thing, beyond dispute; and as such it is entitled to rank within the sum of knowledge.

Somewhat anxiously it may be argued that a soldier in battle finds cause to worry about particular hand-grenades which come sailing towards him with the pins out, and show every sign of being real. Nevertheless it is the *form*, as presented in the particular immediacy of the hand-grenade, which urges the soldier to take shelter. A baby, a chimpanzee or a mental deficient might not bother, they have not learned to recognize the form.

The universe to be seen as a result of platonic doctrines is essentially (1) a world of forms, (2) a featureless stuff in which forms are manifested, and (3) the familiar world of successive, physical and particular instances. (3) may be seen as (1) exemplified or manifested in (2). Knowledge of world (3) is only possible with reference to world (1). Disciplined structures, such as physical science, logic or mathematics, guide the mind into awareness of this—away from the controversial particular to the settled universal—and especially, according to Plato, towards the contemplation of the highest form of all, which is that of the Good.

To turn to Whitehead's account, universals are seen in his philosophy as 'forms of definiteness'. They make up collectively 'the realm of possibility'; in other words, everything that can possibly be envisaged. It is not, as for Plato, the realm of completest reality. The only actualities in Whitehead's analysis are the fleeting occasions, and there is literally nothing else.

Whitehead uses the expression 'Eternal Objects' when he

discusses universals. Eternal Objects are mental ingredients within an occasion. The other ingredients are physical. The twin types of ingredient make up the experience of an occasion. We have already noticed the occasion as a kind of magnet having a mental and physical pole. The fundamental relationship of feeling holds between one occasion and another, or between one occasion and an Enternal Object.

The Eternal Objects partake of *prospective* reality, i.e. they *may* be exemplified in some occasion. This is the familiar condition of something that is a possibility. An occasion is a definite degree of feeling, and it is definite because of the presences and relations of the Eternal Objects which enter into it. There is as little sense in visualizing an occasion without the Eternal Objects as there is in imagining a song without music and rhythm. It is the stress of sound, extended in duration, which makes a song, and as with the occasions, it is the wholes or unities into which the sounds are gathered that further the growth of feeling.

The Eternal Objects form an interconnected hierarchy, like a totally conceptual range of colours in the mind of a paint manufacturer. If anyone asked him about one of the colours he could give *some* account of it by saying in effect, 'It's not exactly cobalt or azure, but a cross between the two.' But in the last resort it would only be possible to dab a bit of the actual colour on to a neutral surface and say, 'Here, see for yourself.' Imagine that an earthman visits an alien planet and finds a race of intelligent beings who live entirely on acids. He tries to tell them about the taste of sugar. They have never heard of it—it does not exist in their world. All he can explain is that sweetness is as far as possible the opposite of sourness, an answer that would mean little to a species which knew no flavours except acidity.

Explanation or description is always of past occasions (those which have undergone transition into objective matters-of-fact) in terms of Eternal Objects. We point to the latter or their relations and rely on shared experience for the effectiveness of the explanation. The Eternal Objects themselves cannot be described except in the form of abstractions; and in this way they tend to be looked at as *sets*, like the ranges of colour considered by the paint manufacturer. In other respects they can only be *felt.* This lucky circumstance for mankind has resulted, amongst other things, in the gorgeous trappings of poetry: simile, imagery, metaphor.

Whitehead has much to say about the relations and limitations of Eternal Objects. The shade of red in an apple can be the same as the colour of a red-hot poker. An Eternal Object is always itself, whenever it appears in an occasion. But despite uniqueness and unchangeability, it is always found in relationship with others. Relations are of the essence of Eternal Objects and involve finely extended shadings and tailings-off. The grinder of colours can produce many shades of red: nature produces many more. These relations with other Eternal Objects are determinate. Even if there is no concrete instance of a cry xy times higher than a bat's, the fact that the cry of the majority of bats is x times higher than top C is not an indeterminate or arbitrary fact. Again, occasions are found in determinate relationships with the Eternal Objects they exemplify. Softness can be met with in flowers, mud and flesh, but not in a block of granite. The Whiteheadian universe, in its creative advance, often seems as filled with pattern, as ordered, as a Roman phalanx or British square.

The above statement that softness cannot be found in granite implies that 'granite' is a symbol for a certain collection of qualities, and it is possible to point to the actualization of these and say '*that* is what the word stands for, and it excludes softness'. The same qualities are enlisted time and again to fill out the symbol 'granite'. This limitation of description, or rationing of Eternal Objects to form the living occasions of experience, suggests that there is no possibility in the universe which is completely indeterminate. In other words, it is not true that *all* things are possible. The novelty that is present in every finite occasion is ultimately a limited novelty. However rich the sonata, however boundless-seeming the gamut and bewildering the changes of key, the work as a whole is confined to a particular notation.

Unlike Plato's Universals, which are supposed to be 'reality' in the highest degree, Whitehead's Eternal Objects make merely grammatical sense apart from actual experience. The Universal is an ideal, the Eternal Object a possibility. Ideals are unchanged in essence whether actualized or not. But a possibility is without a completed being except in so far as it may be actualized.

Because each Eternal Object occupies a determinate relation with others, and can be reckoned as item in a series, it enjoys a multiplicity of cross-relationships. These form the aspects under which it can be actualized, e.g. a certain shade of grey may be white darkened or black whitened. Although an Eternal Object can only be experienced in an actual occasion, which usually implies a physical, as well as a mental side, to the resulting feeling, it may be known conceptually by reference to its determinate position in an appropriate series; for, as we have pointed out, it is possible to know *something* of a shade of colour by learning its position on a colour chart. This procedure, of course, would itself involve living occasions and Eternal Objects: there is no escape from the concrete actualities in Whitehead.

It has been said above that each occasion stands in determinate relation with the Eternal Object it exemplified. This could not be otherwise: it is circular nonsense to say that the character of an occasion depends on its character. But the converse relation —between the Eternal Object and the occasion—is one of indeterminacy. It is not the necessary condition of an Eternal Object to be actualized in any particular occasion. If I am expecting a letter and get a postcard, that does not to any extent alter the status of letters as possibilities in general.

It is often held that thought is boundless. But whatever is boundless is without shape or perceptible form. It is probable that people who assert that thought is boundless spend most of their time acting the opposite. For Kant, the bounds were imposed by the thinking subject through his essential nature. For Whitehead they are imposed by an ultimate irrationality, a limitation of possibility. Creativity implies precisely such a limitation, and every occasion is an expression of it. Given an initial state in which everything is possible, creativity must of necessity consist of a limiting operation. Such would be the condition of anything coming into being at all.

The above is the character of creativity in action, but, of course, we understand the notion of an *abstract* creativity which is boundless. Whitehead takes this as a final universal principle, an abstract umbrella over his philosophy that cannot be characterized. It is actual only *in so far* as there are actualities.

We have been visualizing Eternal Objects in their more simple examples, such as shades of colour. But like the occasions, which are seen in Whitehead's analysis as atomistic in character and grouped into societies to form 'things', the Eternal Objects are found both singly and in groups of every type of complexity. A particular shade of colour is simple. A state of being, such as 'humanity', is complex.

It has been recalled above that philosophers found grounds for denying the reality of 'substance' in the fact that nothing tangible remained after stripping an object of its qualities. Armed with Whitehead's analysis it is possible to pursue this argument to the extent that the qualities take on the aspect of well-nigh infinite relativity, and the 'substance' that is supposed to reside behind or within them grows even more remote. Every occasion invokes many simple Eternal Objects. Take, for instance, a vase with its particularities of size, colour and shape. In getting actualized in an occasion involving the vase as 'objective datum', the Eternal Objects embark upon a tremendous number of relationships, invoking an equally impressive share of their fellows of greater complexity. Such complexities are the multitudinous sensory aspects of the vase, fused with the historic past of the subject of vases in general, which collectively give rise to the final unity of the occasion. In defining that unity even the Eternal Objects *which do not enter* must be included. Whatever is *not* present is a formative element in the data actually assembled. In this sense the whole universe is represented in each occasion. This is perfectly understandable as a poetic notion. It is also an example of Whitehead's concern to knock down the intellectual fence of bifurcation. Poet and scientist breathe the same air. What is felt is real, is nature itself.

4. PROPOSITIONS: TRUTH

Traditional logic has to do with statements which can either be true or false: in a word, with propositions. A proposition is an assertion, as distinct from a question or command, e.g. 'All men are egotists,' 'All dogs are quadrupeds.' Men and dogs are the 'logical subjects' of these examples; egotists and quadrupeds are the things 'predicated' of the subjects.

When propositions are examined in the light of Whitehead's analysis it will be noticed that each involves a reference, on the one hand, to some Eternal Objects (e.g. 'egotism') and on the other, to some actual occasion or group (e.g. 'all men'). Egotism is here the possibility for the subjects of the proposition. Without a reference to the definite group conjured in 'all men' we cannot attach meaning to the possibility.

There is a type of proposition which refers to a specific event. Whitehead takes the Battle of Waterloo as an example. In this, or any other historic happening, there are possibilities which were not actualized at the time, e.g. Napoleon might have won instead of Wellington. It is clear that the possibilities which surround an event like the Battle of Waterloo are neither (a) general, in the sense in which we understand an Eternal Object to be general, nor (b) particular, in the sense in which an occasion is particular. They may be said to fall between the two. They are Eternal Objects restricted to a particular field of fact. The group of Eternal Objects associated with the Battle of Waterloo are called propositional. All possibilities that are grouped around and confined to any actual fact, whether realized in the fact or not, are *propositions*. Whitehead's stretching of the meanings of familiar words is here extended to a logical term.

One can think of possibilities without reference to any occasion in which they may be actualized, e.g. 'He weareth a runcible hat.' Such are 'pure' conceptual feelings. But a feeling in which a proposition is object—being turned towards some particular actual occasion or group—is what Whitehead calls an '*impure*' conceptual feeling.

Eternal Objects and propositions are definite constituents of Whitehead's universe—features of the 'receptacle' (in platonic language) or potentialities for the 'spacetime continuum' (in the language of our century). They depend nevertheless upon realization in some actual occasion; apart from that they are tangible only in the way that rules of syntax are tangible. Whitehead's scheme of Eternal Objects and propositions can be likened to a competition in which the prize, say, is a trip to a holiday resort. The prize cannot be said to exist in the sense that something like a particular football trophy exists; it cannot be actualized until it has been won and is being enjoyed. Yet for the competitors it is an objective possibility to be realized. The objective character of the competition is conditioned by the prize, as similarly, the objectivity of the whole universe is conditioned by its finite possibilities.

On a sceptical view of things propositions are often taken to be identical with subjective judgments, e.g. if I make the statement that 'all men are egotists' I am saying less about men than about myself. As we have seen, in Whitehead's stretching of the term, 'proposition' is defined as something available to be experienced. The Eternal Object 'egotist' is invoked and coupled with the living occasions, 'all men'. The result is an objective entity, which, as already noted, is changed into a subjective unity of feeling. It does not matter whether all men are egotists or not, truth is irrelevant to process. Lies are felt occasions, as well as truth.

Whiteheadian propositions need never be verbally stated. Written and spoken language can only symbolize reflections of the real world; the group of Eternal Objects which form a propositional complex around any occasion is always too multitudinous for expression. In fact, the majority of propositions are unconscious or entertained in feeling without knowledge. We know that the physical feelings of 'dead' things are such that the data is largely repeated. A living occasion, on the other hand, entertains Eternal Objects in addition to the bare 'given' data. If there are felt possibilities, felt potentialities, to that extent an occasion contains a propositional complex. The successive feelings created in a reader by the printed page have reference to such a complex. It is an enrichment of the bare physical feelings engendered by the impact of light from the printed page to the optic nerves.

Reference should be made here to Whitehead's way of characterizing a further group of the components of experience, i.e. mathematical entities, such as points, lines, instants. His method is relational and employs the aspect of duration, as it well must if experience is to be analysed in terms of the event. As this topic, in the scheme adopted for this book, fits more neatly into the account of Space and Time, its introduction has been delayed until the next Chapter.

It is evident that Whitehead wreaks havoc amongst the venerable pages of formal logic. What, for example has happened to the element of 'judgment'? When I 'judge' anything a proposition is always there. But it is not itself the judgment.

NEW SHAPES OF REALITY

Traditionally a sentence like 'all men are egotists' is taken to be proposition and judgment. This is not so in Whitehead's system, and the difference is worth further discussion.

In a propositional feeling, the proposition, which is conceptual, is the objective datum to be felt. Judgment does not usually enter such a feeling. As we know, the vast majority of feelings are unconscious. Even where propositional feelings exist in full consciousness, judgment does not usually enter.

It may be asked what a proposition is if it is not a judgment; for 'all men are egotists' looks very much like one. In his set course of generalizing about everything until the ultimate generality is reached, Whitehead, as we have noted, has enlarged the definition of 'proposition' so that the objective datum to be felt—'all men'—may be coupled with a plural possibility— 'egotists'. *Judgment* becomes the question of whether the possibilities *really* conform with the datum. It is obvious that I may experience the proposition without judging. The propositional feelings of the world are rarely to be called judging occasions.

It is when one is faced with an *oral* proposition that judgment stands more chance of being brought in. But even here the chances are against it. Most written material is propositional, yet readers are rarely constrained to judge, and the probability of judgment lessens as the aesthetic quality of the material increases. Whitehead offers here the example of Hamlet's soliloquy beginning 'To be or not to be, that is the question.' Few are interested in judging whether this be true or false; it is enjoyed in feeling for its own sake.

When occasions of judgment *do* occur they would appear to be mainly conscious and intellectual—markedly different from propositional feelings. In the latter the proposition is the datum felt. A judgment is not what is felt; it is identical with the subject, the 'feeler'. In such an occasion the objective datum is twofold. On the one hand it consists of a proposition, entertained as an idea, and on the other it is a physical feeling. Judgment is an intellectual synthesis of these two parts of the datum whereby the conceptual part is compared with the physical part.

Since childhood, let it be assumed, I have known that Roman roads are straight. This proposition has been the objective datum in some of my feelings about roads. When, for the first time, I find myself on a real Roman road, I begin, also for the first time, to make a judgment about them. This is a feeling in which both the proposition 'All Roman roads are straight' and the solid road in front of me are present as objective data. The conformity or otherwise between the conceptual proposition and the physical road determine the conclusion of judgment. If I find a perfectly straight road before me I am entitled to assume that the proposition may be true. It does, of course, speak of 'all' Roman roads, and this is only one road. It may at least be said that the feeling realized in my judgment is coherent.

But what, after all, is truth?

Judgments are subjective feelings which consist of a comparison between two elements—a proposition and a physical fact—within the experience of the feeler. In so far as the result seems coherent or incoherent, or if it can be acted on successfully or verified by physical experiment, it must be acceptable in many cases as 'truth'. But truth or falsity mean more than this to a great many, who might maintain that there is an absolute sense in which propositions correspond with reality, even if no individual has known or can ever know their truth in this sense. We have seen that a proposition is an objective datum on the one hand and an Eternal Object, or group of such, on the other. Its truth or falsity—the *precise* degree of correspondence between datum and Eternal Object—must surely exist, it would seem, without reference to any individual feeling!

By this time the reader should be able quickly to answer that ideas of actualities apart from individual feelings do not occur in Whitehead. It would be well, at this stage, to look at the concept of truth more closely.

Truth is a relation between appearance and reality, or between something felt conceptually and a physical fact. The world's facts are in themselves neither true nor false; they are just 'given'.

Traditionally a proposition is held to be true when the appropriate relation or correspondence obtains between subject and predicate. If 'egotists' is *really* exemplified in 'all men', then men are egotists. In practice no one can test this—no one knows all men. But all men are either egotists or they are not. As a matter of faith in the sanity of things it seems proper to maintain that the universe must include somewhere the elements of whatever proposition it is that expresses the possibilities of all men being egotists. Also, of course, the truth about everything—

what song the sirens sang—what planets have orbited other suns. This, essentially, is the meaning of one of the three principal theories of truth, the Correspondence Theory. This, the theory of commonsense, says that a proposition is true if there is some fact or situation having elements which not only correspond with its terms, but have a structure which to an accurate degree mirrors those terms. There are propositions which it is theoretically possible to verify. Many modern supporters of some form of correspondence theory hold that propositions may be 'true', 'false' or 'nonsensical'. These last are the theoretically unverifiable, and many would call it nonsense to ask whether anything corresponds with them or not.

Some might hold that no person knows, or can ever know, the facts. Therefore it is never possible to know the truth. If it is held that an object is nothing but the sum of its relationships with others (which sum is well-nigh infinite), or that the universe is indivisible and cannot be understood by studying arbitrarily-selected 'bits', then it would seem wrong to assert the truth of any proposition except the one which expresses the assertions. In that case the only 'true' proposition would be of the nature of one posed by God about Himself. Therefore (carping philosophers would say) the correspondence theory, by definition, is beyond human scope, even if it should happen to be metaphysically valid; and that what occurs in practice is a crude realism with provisional truth postulated of 'facts' which are make-shift abstractions from the unknowable. So the correspondence of fact with idea is but an improbable dream and cannot be what philosophers mean when they speak of truth.

A little less radical is that approach to the concept of truth which looks to the character of coherence. Those who think of the universe as an indivisible whole are bound by their premises to give up the idea that a fact is coherent in isolation. Accordingly many can, and do, go further and say that there are no such things as facts—that there is no truth available to provide the goal of judgment. What we call a fact, on this showing, is a limited idea—something nearly meaningless until an adequate account is given of its context. But in the last resort its context is the Absolute, and as we can neither know the Absolute nor make metaphysical sense of an isolated fact, it follows that truth must always lie beyond us. How then do we manage to live successfully *at all*? Because, it is answered, we look habitually for coherence and significance rather than absolute truth.

This means that we often know a *certain number* of related facts, even if we cannot know the total. Whatever degree of truth we are entitled to claim for our judgment depends on the extent of that knowledge. There is a degree of truth in the judgment that the earth moves 'round' the sun. But the matter gains in significance when it is known that the roundness is not circular but elliptical, and that there is a 'wobble' at certain times. The significance increases when the context is widened to bring in gravitation, and again there is an increase when the spacetime continuum replaces the classical type of space. Even now the judgment is not *reality*—for that one would need a finished metaphysics—but it has become increasingly more coherent than the original statement that the earth moves round the sun.

There is another sense in which isolated facts are held to fall short of reality and their mere collection insufficient as an approach to truth. A whole is greater than its parts. There is something about a chair which is significant over and above the items of which it is made. It is a particular grouping within a universe that may be described for this purpose as 'not-chair'. A chair is a 'whole', a resting place for the understanding no less than for the posterior. Now it can be imagined that an intelligent worm has discovered that the distance through one of the legs is thirty times that of its own body. The worm is ignorant, however, of the nature of its environment, i.e. of chair legs and of chairs. The worm's judgment will have been 'true' in a limited sense, a sense far less significant than it would have been if some awareness of the chair in its wholeness had entered. Even if they show some formal kind of truth, judgments are incomplete in proportion with their failure to note a context. In ever-widening generality, 'wholes' surround any fact like ripples. The noting of these is the measure of coherence, and it is the degree attained that proportions the value of truth.

According to this theory, a completed truth cannot be found short of the Absolute; all our dealings involve truths that are incomplete, and judgments stand or fall on the degree of their coherence. It is doubtful if many modern people think habitually on such lines. A pragmatic approach is more common.

Imagine that the universe as it 'really' exists is a featureless flux or continuum which is split up by the mind into the things and relations with which we have to do. The way in which the things are abstracted depends on the sort of mind that makes the abstraction. Ultimately the criteria by which things are distinguished by the mind from the flux is nothing more than their *usefulness*. That a thing 'makes sense' is another way of saying that it aids the act of living.

There are many theories as to how the world comes to be perceived. Pre-Kantean philosophers would have it that we never actually perceive objects as unified wholes, but entertain multitudes of impressions and ideas, such as hardness, softness, etc. In Kant's version, these bewildering atomies are 'worked up' by the mind and unified into a concrete world of experience.

Such an account might easily be reversed. Far from unifying a world that is 'really' fragmentary, the mind might be engaged in making fragments of something that is 'really' a unity. No one would achieve anything if all were featureless and unified. The introduction of a mind means that an agent has appeared capable uniquely of making distinctions. In the mind's absence the universe would continue to be a well-nigh featureless whole.

The pragmatic theory of truth is not inconsistent with such a metaphysical background, although on pragmatism's own showing it is fair to say that the 'truth' of any account of reality must undergo a test which it is sometimes hard to apply. If the objects and relations selected by the mind are precisely those which make a concrete and liveable world, the beliefs which the mind entertains must themselves contribute. We are prone to accept as true those ideas that satisfy us emotionally, and to confirm their truth if they are found to 'work', i.e. lead to successful action. In pragmatism it is the degree of workableness that distinguishes truth from untruth. The test of success in practice is the proper guide to truth's *meaning*. A proposition is true if it is a success.

Classical philosophy was concerned with the pursuit of wisdom through the acquisition of knowledge, and would have regarded the question 'So what?' as irrelevant, if not irreverent. But many philosophers of our own time have concerned themselves with this question. Pragmatically the answer is in terms of human utility or happiness, to which end knowledge and wisdom can only be instrumental. It is apt that this distinctive view is sometimes called Instrumentalism.

The central ideas of pragmatism derive from C. S. Peirce. They were elaborated by William James. We should not struggle after absolute truth. All that is necessary is to ask ourselves what practical effects follow from assumptions. That the iceberg is cold or the fungi poisonous are not in themselves statements of value; they add to the wisdom of nobody until they become instruments for effective action. In summary, as Bertrand Russell puts it, pragmatism holds that a belief is true when its effects are good.

Thus the correspondence theory defines truth as correspondence with fact. The coherence theory either denies that facts exist in isolation or dismisses them as unknowable, and defines truth as a harmony between one idea and others that have been abstracted from an essential oneness. Finally in pragmatism all absolutism is given up: truth is a tried and tested mental construction that has been applied to the world—a construction dictated by the necessity of living to advantage.

Whitehead seems both to accept and reject these three theories. The truth of a proposition lies in its relation with the group of actual occasions which is its logical subject. A and B have a truth-relation if their composite natures include a common factor. The proposition is true when the group of facts, of which something is being asserted, does in reality exemplify the pattern which is the predicate of the proposition.

The subjective feeling of an occasion arises from a settled fact. It is when we begin to ask whether the properties we feel are also properties of the settled fact, apart from our feeling, that the question of truth becomes relevant.

In higher organisms the settled fact with which experience starts is worked upon to such an extent that another fact with many different qualities emerges. I experience what Whitehead calls a 'nexus' of occasions with a certain physical feeling as objective datum; I mix a conceptual feeling with the given material. I experience, say, a Louis Quatorze chair. The raw data, the chair, has been transformed in the occasion to an element in a proposition. The chair is what it is and constitutes reality in the most definite sense. But the data which collectively make up the chair might not constitute a *Louis Quatorze* chair at all. They might constitute a Queen Anne chair, or even a trick of light and shadow that leads me to imagine a chair to be present in a room which contains only tables. Be that as it may, they are 'worked over' by subjective feelings which integrate them with ideas (i.e. Eternal Objects) all featuring Louis Quatorze; and whatever emerges from the occasion is something quite different from the raw data. Reality has become appearance. Certain configurations, in themselves mere 'hurrying of material', have become a Louis Quatorze chair. The mental world has merged with the physical and produced a proposition where before existed a raw physical feeling.

Appearances are 'true', according to Whitehead, if they correspond with the given physical data. The Whiteheadian expression is 'conformity'. The theory at this stage is a version of the correspondence theory. This may suggest that the truth-relation obtains between something already existing (reality) and a subjective feeling (appearance); but such a simplification does not quite meet the complexity of Whitehead's occasions.

Something physical is given, and subjective feeling constructs a Louis Quatorze chair. But before there can be any judgment, the subjective feelings have to reach their unity and themselves be experienced *objectively* as a fact. Only then can they be tested for conformity with the initial fact.

It follows that truth is an Eternal Object which cannot achieve meaning until it enters into some actual occasion; and *then* it is found to be inapplicable to a single feeling but to be a relation (which can, of course, itself be 'felt' in the Whiteheadian sense) between two feelings, the initial physical data and the conceptual proposition.

Appearance that is presented as a proposition is felt as a *possibility*. This is not so in more predominately physical occasions. As far as such are concerned there are fewer elements of possibility—there is forthright table, chair or tree demanding recognition. The Whiteheadian type of correspondence theory applies to these no less than to the more conceptual feelings: truth is affirmed if what we *think* we see has elements in common with what is already 'there'.

An exact conformity between object and idea is probably rare. In this respect Whitehead differs strictly from the correspondence theory in that he demands no complete conformity. Take, for example, the relation between a healthy organism and its environment. I may feel the weather to be mild, whilst my older and more feeble neighbour complains of the cold. Inasmuch as I am healthy, my perception must be in a certain relation of truth with the environment; for I am a normal member of a species; the environment 'threw up' that species: therefore there must be some sort of conformity between myself and the environment.

The precise degree of correspondence with fact in any proposition is a matter for conjecture; one supposes a greater or less degree according to the 'normality' of the organ of feeling. Here is a familiar situation, i.e. the necessity for pragmatism. Although correspondence with reality is admitted to be the meaning of truth, the degree can never accurately be revealed by comparative method. So Whitehead adopts pragmatism without defining truth ultimately as pragmatic. For the normal organism, whatever 'works' and aids process is true. Nevertheless, the metaphysical *meaning* of truth is correspondence with reality. This point is probably the nearest Whitehead ever got to his own anathema of bifurcation.

CHAPTER FOUR

THE SPACETIME CONTINUUM

1. CLASSICAL SPACE

Where do the intensive relations of Whitehead's organisms *happen*? In what sort of receptacle, frame of reference or space-time continuum is process to be located?

In spite of our understanding that Whitehead's scheme is not 'science', and is fruitfully to be seen as an analysis of experience from a new viewpoint designed to eliminate the philosophical conundrums of the past, the question posed above is a proper one. The same asked of Ptolemy or Aristotle would have produced a description of the Celestial Sphere; of Newton, the absolute mechanical universe; of Einstein, the relativistic and finite field of spacetime. None of these scientific systems would provide a stage for our experience as analysed by Whitehead. Therefore we are entitled to ask the question; and Whitehead, in fact, has devoted himself to answering it.

The need for a receptacle—'space' to modern minds—was recognized by Plato. In addition to ideas (the universal forms) and individual phenomena (the particular instances of the forms), Plato saw a third existent, 'the seat of becoming'. This receptacle is not quite the same as our 'space', since it is featureless, while modern 'space' has geometrical properties. It was seen by Plato as something available to understanding without the aid of the senses. It was absolutely essential to the existence of phenomena. Such phenomena—objects of sensation, in themselves merely the appearances of something else—must have some supporting or reflecting medium before they can come into being. The universal forms were outside 'space'. 'Space' was the mirror that reflected them in experience in the guise of individual phenomena. It was a case of no mirror, no phenomena.

For Plato, individual phenomena were the products of the creative demiurge, Who exemplified the forms in the 'receptacle'. Accordingly, Plato's universe requires three bases:

(i) The universal forms,

(ii) God (the demiurge) in Whose apprehension the forms have their being,

(iii) Space (the receptacle) in which exist the phenomena, the disorderly world of becoming.

Time, like space, is taken to be a necessity for the world of the phenomena, but not for the 'real' world of the forms. The latter are eternal and unchanging; the phenomena on the other hand, change and perish. Time and space are the receptacle for those reflections of Plato's universal forms which comprise the everyday world.

Broadly speaking, the classical philosophers were concerned with ideas, and reasoned from those to the particular events with which human life has to do. Later thought—scientific and empirical—began with the *events* and tried to sort these into ideas. Some historians of philosophy trace this redirection to the Nominalists of the twelfth century. Nominalism and Realism were two opposing views of mediaeval scholastic philosophy. The Realists held, with Plato, that the universal forms were alone 'real' and that all particular phenomena were reflections or shadows of them. The Nominalists disagreed, holding that the so-called forms were nothing but names for classes of things, and that the things themselves, in their multiplicity, made up whatever was real.

It seems probable that experimental science as we know it could not have arisen from the platonic or Realist doctrine. In the event, the scientific method not only arose—it became separated from the main stream of philosophy. It is sometimes forgotten that 'science' is a fairly new notion. In the past, science and philosophy meant the same thing. The goal of modern theoretical science, the principles behind phenomena—is identical with what classical philosophy was supposed to be seeking.

In deserting philosophy, science formed a new liaison. It is not only concerned with abstract principles, but also with problems of getting good results from particular situations, providing the fount of washing machine and television set. It is this side of science that is in course of ousting wisdom as a human aim.

Modern ideas of space and time, scientific methods as a whole, and in some sense Whitehead's philosophy as well, owe much to the seventeenth- and eighteenth-century philosophers known as the empiricists. A brief sampling of their climate, before we enter the more rarified atmosphere of relativistic spacetime, will clear the way for Whitehead's own proposals to modify the dimensional universe.

We have seen that the impressions of the five senses are by no means the sole sources of knowledge. Our feelings of past, present and future, included in a faculty of ours which Whitehead calls 'causal efficacy', must also be admitted. Again, every occasion is an organism having a mental as well as a physical pole, and Whitehead does not suggest that the ideas we entertain—his 'Eternal Objects'—enter primarily by way of the senses, but arise as conceptual feelings, allied to the solid notes of the physical world somewhat in the style of overtones in music. When physical feelings enter they drag a relational gift of ideas with them.

The above is one philosopher's way of interpreting experience. Most people have a decided theory of the kind of world they inhabit and would agree that the feelings derived from the bodily senses do not seem to give much 'clue' as to the nature of that world. So far short do they fall that we are left wondering how we come to find ourselves with knowledge. How have we gained it? Is it trustworthy? If not, can we find some faculty that will replace it with other, more valid knowledge? Perhaps it is 'commonsense' that has given us knowledge, a notoriously faulty faculty according to philosophers, scarcely one of whom, apparently, can speak of it without a sneer. In that case, maybe, we should search for some more elegant instrument—the speculative reason, the mysterious faculty that gives us a priori convictions—even religious or aesthetic feeling?

From the start of 'modern' philosophy much emphasis was placed on the rôle of reason as the provider of knowledge. The argument depended on a theory that people were born with certain faculties already implanted in their minds, and that knowledge did not come so much by way of the senses as by using those faculties, i.e. by 'reasoning'. The question of a priori knowledge—that a person could, in theory, puzzle out the whole of mathematics from 'two twos are four'—has been mentioned before; it was held by Descartes and other 'rationalist' philosophers that all general truths were of this nature and could be worked out by the unaided reason from elementary principles.

This may certainly apply, it might be said, to 'necessary' facts —the type which 'could not be otherwise', like the fact that two plus two equals four. But what about other types of fact which the universe manifestly contains? Men have two legs in London, but in some Venusian city they might have three. Even if this last fact were true, it is not 'necessary'. It could well be otherwise: Venusians might have five legs.

In the face of such difficulties some rationalist philosophers proceeded to call all facts 'necessary' and thus available for discovery by reason. Nothing in the universe appeared capable of being other than it was; and from such a philosophical atmosphere Voltaire drew the model for Pangloss, with his doctrine that everything was for the best in the best of all possible worlds.

The rationalists were opposed by the empiricists, who demoted reason and acclaimed observation as the main instrument of knowledge. This is more like the outlook of a modern man of science. The existence of most facts, they contended, could not be inferred by reason, only by observation and experiment. Reason could help at a later stage by saying what should follow from the factual situation discovered by observation, but it could not be substituted for observation itself, which 'boiled down' to sense experience.

The empiricists of the past have become the scientists of the present. The rationalists have vanished; in present usage a 'rationalist' is one who denies supernatural agencies. Those like Locke and Newton who held that information obtained from sense-data is the main source and content of knowledge, laid the foundations of the impedimenta of modern life.

The history of scientific inquiry often suggests a modification of strict empiricism. The more searching the effort, the more it appears that recourse has to be had to conclusions not 'given' in sense-experience, but arrived at by way of the speculative reason. Newton is perhaps a case in point. Particular as he was in stressing that his business was with the causes of sensible effects, and that where experimental evidence was lacking he would frame no hypothesis, he had still to attach a meaning to things not given by the senses, e.g. the notions of absolute space, time and motion.

'The motions of bodies included in a given space,' wrote Newton, 'are the same among themselves whether that space is at rest or moves uniformly forward in a straight line.' In implication this means that the laws of motion apply as much in one place as in another, and are the same, assuming that the one place is in uniform motion relative to the other.

'Relative' is not a satisfying term if nothing much else is to follow. Somewhere, the brain insists, there must be a fixed point of reference, something in the universe that does not move. But the searching for such a reference is formidable. People move about the earth; the earth rotates on its axis and moves round the sun; the whole solar system moves locally within the galaxy; the galaxy is in motion relative to the rest of the universe which appears in its remoter systems to be receding from the observer at a terrific speed. Obviously it is impossible to say that there are not even more examples of material in motion relative to ourselves.

But perhaps *space itself* could be assigned the rôle of something absolutely at rest, against which the relative motions of material bodies could be measured and their 'true' or absolute motion assessed? It is tempting to think of space as 'something', for space has a function— namely, to separate material bodies by distance—and it is hard to assign any sort of function to 'nothing'.

The notion of absolute space is an important feature of the Newtonian scheme. Modern relativity gives it no place. It provides a prime example of 'bifurcation'; and the point is rammed home when Newton distinguishes between the space and time of ordinary life and of physical science. He writes '. . . the common people conceive these quantities (i.e. time, space, place and motion) under no other notions but from the relation they bear to sensible objects. And thence arise certain prejudices, for the removing of which it will be convenient to distinguish them into absolute and relative, true and apparent, mathematical and common. Absolute, true and mathematical time, of itself, and from its own nature, flows equably, without relation to anything external, and by another name is called duration: relative, apparent and common time, is some sensible and external (whether accurate or unequable) measure of duration by the means of motion. . . .'

More simply: absolute time flows of itself whether we are present or not. If we want to measure time for ourselves we have to make use of something in motion, e.g. a pendulum, hour glass. etc. Similar accounts are given by Newton of absolute space, rest and motion.

Why are absolute frames of reference necessary to Newtonian physics? According to his kinematic theory of atoms, every atom is moving, a statement that would create difficulties if concepts of motion were relative. Again, his first law of motion, which asserts that any object not acted upon by external forces has a constant velocity, seems of itself to require absolute space; for such an object would have to be the only one in the universe, since any other, by Newton's second law, would exert forces on it; and on a relational theory of space the idea of a solitary object in motion is meaningless. There are several other arguments which point in the same direction, and any relational theory must take account of them.

2. 'MODERN' SPACE

During the centuries following Newton the apparent functions of space began to multiply with wavular theories of the propogation of light and electromagnetic phenomena in general. A wave presupposes a medium. To talk of an ocean wave without admitting an ocean to go with it is authentically the idea of the Cheshire Cat in *Alice*. So the theory of the 'ether' was born: briefly, a universal, fixed, jelly-like substance in which the vibrations of electromagnetics and the motions of material bodies could be accommodated.

The idea of 'action at a distance', e.g. the observable actions of magnets and of light rays in a vacuum, seemed impossible without such a medium as the ether. Yet an experiment performed in the USA in 1881, the result of which has never been challenged, yielded the surprising information that the apparent velocity of the earth through the ocean of ether was nil. In other words, there was either no ether or the earth was not in motion. Of these alternatives science chose the first, and looked elsewhere for the carrier-medium required by electrodynamics.

The experiment mentioned, known as the Michelson-Morley experiment, rang the death-knell of 'absolute' space. One of the incidental conclusions was that the velocity of light does not change with the motion of the source. If I shine a torch into space *against* the earth's motion, the velocity of the beam is the same as if I had shone the torch *with* that motion, in spite of the fact that the beam has gained, in the second case, a 'gift' of motion of about a thousand miles an hour. Yet if I fire a revolver from the front of a moving train the speed of the bullet is increased by the speed of the train.

In 1905 Einstein published his first theory of relativity. Einstein's work is in essence a mathematical description of the laws of nature. It does not contradict Newton's system, but embraces that system with greater generality. The result is that Newton's system is practical and valid for applying to small parts of the universe, but when it comes to immense distances and speeds it is Einstein's system which applies with greater accuracy. But whereas the Newtonian universe can be conjured up as vividly as a sewing machine, Einstein's is unimaginable in concrete or mechanical terms; it is a system to be described mathematically or else vaguely grasped by minds well trained in the theatre of the absurd.

Crudely, the main tenets of relativity are as follows. Newton's own relativity principle, quoted above, is enlarged to include all the laws of nature. Thus it is not only the motions of bodies that are the same in uniformly moving systems—Einstein includes light, 'radio waves' and radiant energy of all kinds. The idea of absolute space is given up, together with that of a body absolutely at rest. This applies to time as well: there are no absolutes for Einstein. Time is subjective; it is simply a local ordering of objects and events. There is no such thing as 'now'. The idea of contemporary events in separate parts of the universe belongs to fantasy.

The speed of light is constant. We do not know why light should always travel at 186,284 miles per second; it is not even a round figure. The ancients yearned after harmony, and the first blow at their shapely and ordered system was struck by Copernicus with his untidy patterns substituted for the perfectly circular planetary paths of the older cosmologies. One wonders what the ancients would have thought of such an ill-bred figure as 186,284.

Lastly we learn in relativity (a) that energy can be expressed in terms of mass and vice versa, i.e. that matter and energy are basically the same; (b) gravitation is not a 'force' or mutual attraction between bodies, but arises from inertia; each body moves along the path of least resistance in obedience to what Bertrand Russell calls 'the law of cosmic laziness'; (c) the universe is a four-dimensional spacetime continuum, time being the fourth dimension.

It follows that the search for anything stationary in the universe must be given up, and the movements of a piece of matter can only be measured by taking some other movement as 'standard'. Space is not a receptacle after all; it has no dimensions in the sense that a box or bucket has dimensions. It has not even *directions*: there is no up, down, sideways. The factors that make possible such things as directions and dimensions are the pieces of matter; *space* is an expression of the various relationships and comparisons it is possible to derive from them.

It is similar with time. Whether one adopts Whitehead's approach or not, the impression an individual has of the world *does* strongly take the form of a series of events or occasions, and if anything definitive can be said about one of these it is that the event in question is 'earlier' or 'later' than another. There seems to be an irreversible time-pattern. But on reflection there are two confusing features of this pattern, i.e.:

(a) *My time-pattern is not yours.* Time, to me, is a private awareness of duration, and your own awareness might be entirely different. I might be a gentleman of advanced age drowsing in a bathchair at the seaside; *you* an infant scampering on the sands. Indeed, the awareness of time need not even be parcelled according to external evidences of youth and age. Whitehead suggests that 'youth' should be defined as 'Life as yet untouched by tragedy'. Be that as it may, the point emerges that, apart from clocks, time is subjective. After stroking an elephant one might pronounce a farm worker's hands to be smooth. Similarly, whilst enjoying an interesting holiday, one thinks of the days as far shorter than equal days on which one was bored. Clocks are devices for lifting time from the class of private feelings and making it a public, objective quantity. Einstein says, 'We understand by a clock something which provides a series of events which can be counted.' We compare our private feelings of duration with the events registered by the clock and order our conduct accordingly; trains are caught, meetings attended and a society is possible.

(b) *There is no absolute 'flow' of time.* If space is to be included in our estimate of reality it must be defined as the relationships which pieces of matter, in our experience, have with each other. And if we wish to include time also, we must define it as the relationships between separate occasions, again within the experience of the individual. All our measurements of time are geared to more or less regular and rhythmic movements of material in space—a pendulum, the earth's solar orbit, etc. These movements are native to our particular habitation, the earth, and if we went elsewhere, to Mars, Venus or outside the solar system altogether, we would have to adopt different standards. But however far we travelled we could never meet a fixed 'flow' or 'pulse' of time apart from the measuring-apparatus provided by whatever movements of material were available. Further, it is meaningless to say that the 'now' derived from our particular measuring-apparatus on earth has any validity beyond our immediate environment. It is high fantasy to look at a distant star and say, 'I wonder what is happening there *now.*' As we all know, the star is so far away that its light may have taken centuries to reach us, and the star may have ceased to exist before Nelson fought at Trafalgar. When we look at an object we are not observing the contemporaneous; and this applies to the vase on the mantelpiece equally with the distant nebulae. Each of us is a lonely person in the contemporary world, and were it not for the lifelines of the past and future, it is certain that the existential aspect of experience would loom even larger in thought than it does today.

Although unnecessary, strictly speaking, to our main theme of Whitehead's philosophy, it is tempting to notice here some other features of mathematical relativity which perennially fascinate the layman. One of Einstein's conclusions, for instance, is that duration (the interval between measurable pulsations) varies in different places according to the speed of the 'system'. A 'system' may be a ship, a train or a whole planet. For example, a clock at an airport is going *faster* than another situated in an aircraft; for the one is located in a system which is moving at a greater speed than the other. This sounds incredible. If true, why does not my watch differ from the station clock when I get off the train? The answer is that the variation is too small for measurement where relatively low speeds are involved; but if the train had been going at something near the speed of light the slowing down would have been obvious. This has been verified by experiment, using a radiating atom as a 'clock'.

Another eccentric character of high speed is *the shrinkage of units of measurement* located in a moving system. It does not matter what the unit is; it could be a ruler, tape measure or simply the distance from my chest to my backbone. A stick travelling at around 160,000 miles per second would shrink to some 50 per cent of its original length in the direction of motion. If it reached the total velocity of light it would dwindle to nothing. A clock in such circumstances would slow down and stop.

The implication of the above, which in spite of the violence offered to commonsense is acceptable to most physicists as a fact of nature, is that nothing can travel faster than light. This has proved an unpalatable truth to writers of science-fiction, for it lengthens interstellar journeys to a tedious extent (the nearest star, apart from the sun, would take more than a decade to reach, even if the spaceship travelled at just below the speed of light). So writers of this school usually pretend that Einstein has been proved wrong and that a greater speed (appropriately called an 'overdrive') has proved possible. Whatever the degree of plausibility in an overdrive, it remains that few writers of fiction could offend commonsense as successfully as nature herself in the laws revealed in relativity.

Doubts about overdrives do not solely depend on the stoppage of clocks and disappearance of measuring rods; it is to another of Einstein's conclusions that we usually turn for an assurance that nothing can travel faster than light. This is the rule that mass increases with the speed of a body, reaching infinity with the speed of light. The faster anything travels, the heavier it gets, and by the time it has reached the limit of possible velocity, the speed of light, it possesses infinite weight. 'Weight' and 'heaviness' are used here in the physicists' sense of 'resistance to a change of motion'.

From the finite velocity of light and the behaviour of the mass of a body Einstein moved to the revolutionary theory that has already transformed our time. Classical science had assumed that the universe contained two separate ingredients, matter and energy. The first was weighty and extended spatially in the form of separated lumps; the second was neither weighty nor confined to a localized existence, but seemed an active and unseen principle which enabled the otherwise inert material to move about. Einstein shows that energy and weight are interchangeable terms, that mass and energy are basically the same. In the last analysis there is no difference in kind between a piece of coal and a unit of electricity; both are mass-energy, and the only difference between them is the physical state in which they happen to be.

If matter and energy are the same, what of other universal 'forces' such as inertia and gravitation? In Newtonian science a body 'continues in its state of rest, or of uniform motion in a straight line, unless it is compelled to change that state by forces impressed thereon'. This is part of the classical law of inertia—the reason for the 'first gear' in a motor car, and why an old engine pants and strains in the effort to accelerate the combined mass of chassis, coachwork and driver. The other part of the law says that the amount of force necessary to accelerate a body depends on the mass of the body. If I take out the seat cushions the mass of the car is less, and it will accelerate with less fuss from the engine.

All this applies to horizontal motion; it is a different matter when bodies are *falling*. All bodies fall at the same rate of acceleration, whether they are feathers or leaden weights; the observable differences in rate are entirely due to air-resistance. So whereas the horizontal velocity of a body depends on the initial push, which in turn is strictly affected by the body's mass, its *vertical* velocity seems to have nothing to do with mass. To remove a ton of rubbish a hundred feet I would require to overcome a ton of inertia, but not if I had an old mineshaft into which the rubbish could be tipped. In such a case gravity would do the work.

Imagine that this scene, featuring the ton of rubbish and the mineshaft, is being enacted on the airless Moon. I tip the rubbish piece by piece into the shaft and note how everything—lumps of stone, splinters, scraps of paper—falls at precisely the same velocity. Why is the stone as 'light' as the paper? What has happened to the law of inertia that operates so inexorably on a horizontal plane?

Newton's law answers that the 'force' with which one body attracts another increases with the mass of the body attracted. The lighter the object, the stronger the pull of gravity, and vice versa. Objects fall at the same rate because gravity is always applied to the exact extent required for overcoming the inertia of the body.

Thus classical science assumed that two properties of nature, gravitation and inertia, always acted together in perfect balance; and the success of modern industrial and engineering 'know-how' bears witness that no more fundamental assumption is necessary as far as many practical activities are concerned. But with the pushing of inquiry into remote space, with greater complexity and interrelation of matter-energy, the old law of gravitation was found less satisfactory. The new gravitational picture is drawn in Einstein's General Theory of Relativity.

Einstein notes that it is not always possible to distinguish between motion produced by inertial and gravitational forces. In fact, he gives up the idea of 'forces', 'action at a distance', 'attraction', etc. The motions of bodies are described, not in terms of any mutual attraction exerted, but in terms of the inertia they possess, which determines the nature of the space around them, i.e. the 'field'.

The existence of a 'field' is not a new discovery. Electrical fields have long been known, and before Einstein was born schoolboys were examining the magnetic field made visible by the use of paper, magnet and iron filings. Einstein concludes that all bodies affect the space around them and cause that space to display distinct properties. Thus the apple does not fall from the tree because it is attracted by the earth's gravitational 'pull'; it is behaving like any other piece of matter caught in a gravitational field. It could no more follow another pattern than could a splinter of iron refuse the design imposed by a magnetic field; and both fields are to be described as convolutions and foldings of space, or more precisely, of a four-dimensional spacetime continuum.

3. WHITEHEAD'S EXTENSIVE CONTINUUM

We have dwelt at length on the theory of relativity, although it cannot be claimed that Einstein presents any spectacular endorsement of Whitehead's picture from the side of physical science. Our reason for reviewing Einstein's work is tactical. Whiteheadian space and time involve such a break with the mechanical model of the universe that it is salutory to remind ourselves that 'official' science has made a break equally as radical already.

The most noticeable thing about the universe as revealed in relativity is the departure from mechanism involved. The modern universe resembles a machine only when you examine certain pieces of it, neither too large nor too small. The smaller bits are inclined to behave in so indeterminate a fashion that the machine-analogy breaks down at once. With the larger bits it is equally unrewarding to seek mechanical analogies. A domain where matter and energy are in basis interchangeable and where material bodies depend for their physical character on their degree of motion, is more like an *organism*. If comparisons are to be made it is surely with animal bodies, with their chemical transmutations, the interaction between mental and physical, the power to blush and shiver.

Einstein's purpose was to describe the behaviour of matter-energy in equations of the widest possible generality. The product of his achievement is a universe that bends back on itself and is 'finite yet unbounded'; a universe which might conceivably be governed by one primaeval principle—some single fundamental that appears to us in many different guises masquerading as 'forces'—gravitation, energy, inertia, electromagnetism, etc.

Einstein's theory does not involve any presentation of a cosmology. The equations are descriptions of laws of nature. As to the identity or meaning of nature we are not informed. A cosmology is a description-plus-explanation. An example is the pre-Copernican description of the heavens in terms of astronomy and theology, with the throne of God located above Jerusalem, as objective as a moored balloon. Another example, never in fact presented, might have been the mechanist system of Newtonian physics plus Newton's own theology as 'explanation'. Whitehead's philosophy also contains that rare edifice, a cosmology. To that extent he is a full member of a club to which Einstein, for all his distinguished genius, did not quite 'belong'. However, there is no doubt that Einstein would have shunned this club.

Whitehead more than once spoke of his admiration for Einstein, although his regard was often coupled with criticism. In a book devoted specifically to relativity (*The Principle of Relativity With Application to Physical Science*) he refers to Einstein's theories as 'a magnificent stroke of genius', but adds, 'The worst homage we can pay to genius is to accept uncritically formulations of truths which we owe to it.'

An interesting reiteration of this view is provided in Lucien Price's *Dialogues of Alfred North Whitehead*. The following are Whitehead's own words spoken in conversation on September 11, 1945, as reported by Mr Price:

'I had a good classical education, and when I went up to Cambridge early in the 1880s my mathematical training was continued under good teachers. Now nearly everything was supposed to be known about physics that could be known—except a few spots, such as electromagnetic phenomena, which remained (or so it was thought) to be co-ordinated with the Newtonian principles. But, for the rest, physics was supposed to be nearly a closed subject. Those investigations to co-ordinate went on through the next dozen years. By the middle of the 1890s there were a few tremors, a slight shiver as of all not being quite secure, but no one sensed what was coming. By 1900 Newtonian physics were demolished, done for! . . . Speaking personally, it had a profound effect on me: I have been fooled once, and I'll be damned if I'll be fooled again! Einstein is supposed to have made an epochal discovery. I am respectful and interested, but also sceptical. There is no more reason to suppose that Einstein's relativity is anything final than Newton's *Principia*. The danger is dogmatic thought.'

The above is typical of Whitehead; and if it has been suggested that such scepticism might with equal justice be directed to his own work, Whitehead would probably have agreed.

From the above it may be imagined that a physical system derived from Whitehead's analysis of experience would be found to differ seriously from one to which the theory of relativity would apply. In general it must be admitted that there is at least one most serious difference. Nevertheless Whitehead's work does not amount to a criticism of Einstein so much as that typical Whiteheadian endeavour, an attempt to reconcile two opposing systems of thought. The systems in this case are the absolutist theories of Newtonian physics and the relativity ushered in by Einstein. We have already noted that Whitehead defines spatio-temporal concepts (points, instants, etc.) not in terms of relations between material objects, but relatively as between *events*. The internal mathematical features of Whitehead's system demand that space itself is not geometrically modified according to material content. Such a modification, it will be recollected, is a definite requirement of relativity.

To come specifically to the mode of extension demanded by Whitehead's system, we should remind ourselves that a continuum is something continuous, but the idea of a continuum can admit the subsidiary notion of divisibility. Like Einstein, Whitehead modifies the absolutism of time and space required by Newtonian physics, but he sees spacetime as a generalized aspect of the actual conditions of the universe.

For Einstein the geometry of the continuum is determined by the local concentrations of matter-energy. Different features are revealed for different observers, and in so far as the features are all relational, it may be said that they depend on observers for actuality. In this sense Einstein's spacetime is ultimately subjective—not that it is in any way dependent on the *mind* of the observer, but on his location and the motion of the system of which he forms a physical part as against other systems.

For Whitehead such a conclusion would hint at the crime of bifurcation. The idea of a 'real' universe of matter and a 'subjective' imposition of spacetime, even in the modified sense referred to, would be repugnant to him. The only things with actuality are the occasions of experience. Naturally a thing possessing actuality must include aspects and potentialities which partake of that actuality without being themselves the complete and actual thing. Thus an occasion has a conceptual side—there is usually an element of pure 'idea' in any actuality—but ideas, divorced from occasions, are but forms of definitions—possibilities. In a somewhat similar sense, Whitehead's space and time are abstractions. This is the only status granted, because spatial and temporal relations are always to be defined in terms of the relations between occasions. The reality behind the abstraction is the full reality of an actual occasion.

To compare in the form of brief statements the three views—two scientific and one metaphysical—discussed above:

(a) *Newtonian Physics*. Time and space are objective features, in an absolute sense, of the material universe, real in themselves.

(b) *Relativity*. Spacetime is a subjective experience of the universe, to be understood as a local set of relations between material objects and events, depending on an observer.

(c) *Whitehead's Philosophy*. Time and space are aspects of the separate occasions which make up the universe. These aspects, in generalized form, comprise *potentially* the extensive continuum in which everything 'happens', and apart from which nothing could happen and be said to be real.

Whitehead's universe, as extended in space and time, is ultimately relativistic, but not under the same mode as Einstein's. The continuum of Einstein is relative to the field, system or state of motion in which the observer happens to be. Whitehead's continuum is relative to the viewpoint of the one particular atomistic occasion in which it is being felt. The Whiteheadian universe is never the same for any two occasions. It cannot be understood (except as an example of *potentiality*) apart from the viewpoint of a particular occasion.

It is easy to see why this is. The actual world (say, a, b, c, d . . .) as it enters into the objective constitution of any occasion x, consists simply of all these other occasions which, with the addition of novelty, make x what it is. Thus from the point of view of x, the actual world consists of the occasions a, b, c, d, and the world must always be defined, if not with reference to x, then with reference to some other occasion.

Change is always with us. From the viewpoint of a single occasion the universe is in process of becoming something else. So the actual being of the universe, as it enters the constitution of an occasion, is *potentiality*. It is potentiality within the common usage of the word, just as our starting this sentence amounts to the potential birth of a full stop.

The human mind is a kind of probe, or fifth limb, unfettered by space, time or logic. It can think seriously of conditions in a spaceship travelling faster than light, in a universe of one electron, or in the fiery core of the sun. If this were not so, it is hard to see how theoretical science or philosophy could have arisen; for in order to adopt the chains of logic and mathematics mankind must first have the imaginative freedom to discover them.

The extensive continuum required by Whitehead is an imaginative construction of this kind. If the universe of one particular occasion is a real potentiality, a generalization of all such potentialities, drawn from the points of view of all the occasions in the universe, will be identical with the continuum Whitehead requires. Its nature will be that of a relational complex. In order to qualify as actuality, anything that happens must draw its ingredients from this complex and find existence in it.

But when we look out of the window—and we must presumably then be looking at Whitehead's continuum—we see what we take to be anything but a potential construction. We see solid objects, objects that look stubbornly like houses and trees existing in dimensional space. We had better call a halt in our discussion until we have paid our respects to Whitehead's theory of perception.

Again we must recall, in order to refute, the mechanical explanation, which involves things simply located and enjoying in common one universe-wide flow of duration.

Such an explanation requires a commonsense view of perception, that what I experience when I have sensations of sight, touch or hearing *is*, say, a cow. For if I *cannot experience* things like cows that are supposed to occupy space, commonsense cannot very well maintain that they are there at all.

However, many philosophers have held that one could not experience a cow or anything else that occupies space. It was *never* cows, etc., that were experienced, only sensations, optical, auditory. There were not even light- or sound-waves to be experienced; those scientific entities could only be *inferred* from the sensations, as indeed it seemed with everything perceived. It was hard to avoid the conclusion that when people saw a certain horned and coloured shape the only means by which they proceeded to entertain that a cow was present lay in inference. They were not experiencing a solid body which chewed grass and gave milk, but only sensations to which they had given the name 'cow'.

Whether there is anything 'there' or not, whether there is even a 'there'—these are questions which have been asked since the dawn of reason.

The theory that the cow is 'put there' by an inference drawn by the mind out of the various sensations, seems implausible, to say the least. Although reflection does suggest that a collection of sensations (sight, smell) is not a cow, and that therefore the bovine existent must be put there by inference, we do not in practice catch ourselves making such inferences. We see the motor car coming straight at us and we jump for the kerb. To talk of inferences in such a case is ridiculous. But it should be noted that the idea of perception is bound up with that of sight; the other senses are prone to be forgotten. What we *see* is an object; we do not commonly regard 'seeing' as the reception of various sensations of light, colour and shape caused by something *other* than the sensations. This habit is not so marked with the remaining senses. We hear a sound. It 'sounded like' a motor horn. We infer a motor car. We encounter a female during a party game in the dark. Such-and-such a shape. A particular perfume. We infer a girl we know. Such examples remove some of the implausibility of the theory that objects extended in space are *inferred* by the mind from sense-data.

Whitehead analyses this situation and denies the above.

We have already met the basic situation of perception in our example above of a woman and a dripping tap. She hears the sound unconsciously; there is no thought in her head remotely connected with water or taps. She would afterwards describe the situation in terms like this: 'I wondered what had been worrying me, and found it was that tap dripping.' It is not easy to experience such happenings except by accident, because thoughts about the sense-data (interpretations, feelings of annoyance or pleasure) are always creeping in, and then the basic situation is destroyed. As we know, Whitehead calls this situation 'presentational immediacy', and earlier philosophers seem to have missed it altogether, although this item in Whitehead's analysis does, perhaps, owe something to the psychology of William James, who also reacted against the tendencies of traditional British empiricism. In general, philosophers took the fact of sense-experience and tried to figure *from that alone* how the universe in all its details could possible be 'inferred'. Whitehead recognizes that sense-experience 'in the raw' is rather rare; it is almost always mixed with physical feelings of causality. And as we have already seen above, when so mixed it becomes something which Whitehead calls 'causal efficacy'.

This is another point about perception: that cause-and-effect is known to us by way of physical feelings as definite as those derived from the five 'physical' senses, which earlier philosophers seem to have missed entirely. The passage from Hume's *Treatise of Human Nature* summarized above treats of cause and effect as an idea arising from experience. Again, the German philosopher Leibnitz considered our human cognisance of cause and effect to be an abstracting of events in series, dictated by our personal convenience, from what is essentially a continuous principle of change, not in itself susceptible of 'splitting' into causes and effects. Kant held that causation was a necessary connection between events, a concept, part and parcel of the machinery of perception; but conceived as a type of *thinking* (the *a priori*), not as a type of *feeling*, as Whitehead proclaims it.

It is not difficult in self-observation to discover 'causal efficacy' operating; but the observation requires also some analysis. The venerable philosophical problem of *sight* has already been discussed, i.e. although it is admissible that one infers a cow from the sound 'moo', the idea of inference being necessary to anyone when he *sees* a cow seems preposterous. Yet although neither animals nor humans behave as if inferences are being drawn—a bull, one believes, acts characteristically towards a cow on sight, and in any case could scarcely be credited with inferential faculties—there still seems to be a problem. Sense-experiences often do impress us as mere *signals* of touch, colour, sound. Something must be signalling—something, one infers, that is occupying space. What is to bridge the gap between signal and source if not inference?

If we stop at the idea of bare or raw sense-experience, e.g. a person seeing a cow whilst day-dreaming, so that the sight does not 'register', we are certainly in a situation that requires inference before anything but the sensations can enter. Such is Whitehead's 'presentational immediacy'; and it is clear that his predecessors did stop at that situation. But in everyday perception we *feel* causality in just as sharply physical a way as we feel the pricking of needles and the slamming of doors. A soldier feels the whine of a bullet and ducks. This has been described as a reflex action, the motor nerves acting independently of the will under a stimulus from impressions made on the sensory nerves. Such a physiological account is one way of describing how the soldier 'without thinking about it' ducks under the bullet—a mechanical description of the same order as the statement 'If a sharp blow is delivered to the front of the machine, a platform ticket will fall out without a coin having engaged the release mechanism.' If the soldier were asked afterwards what made him duck, he might answer, 'a bullet'. Now the experience cannot be analysed into (a) feeling the whine of the bullet, and (b) ducking. Any attempt to do so would leave the sort of gap between (a) and (b) that is intolerable to philosophy. But it is surely meaningful to say that the soldier feels the bullet *making* him duck. It is an efficacious cause, a bit of the world-process in action resulting in the actuality of feeling.

The same causal efficacy is present in less alarming examples of sense-experience. When we look at a picture we get a complex feeling, but part of the feeling is that we are *seeing the picture with the eyes*. We see the picture 'because' we have eyes; we *feel* the agent of the optical impressions, namely our eyes. Similarly we feel all our other sense organs *implicated* as ingredient to the whole business of cause-and-effect in physical experience; until it seems queer in retrospect that philosophers searched so painfully for psychological or conceptual links, whilst failing to notice that the link was already present in organic feeling. And this not only for 'consciousness'. A bull, we have remarked, cannot with a straight face be described as *inferring*. All things that dimly grope and advance and withdraw, says Whitehead—bulls, jellyfish, plants—show some perception of causal relationship with the world beyond themselves.

It is important to realize that two distinct *modes* of perception are here suggested, presentational immediacy and causal efficacy. The one belongs to observation, the other to knowledge. Whitehead holds that scientific observation must be, and always is, based on the mode of presentational immediacy. while the formulation of laws or theories are necessarily to be expressed in the sort of terms that could only be available through causal efficacy. Newton's apple could be one example and his gravitational law the other. It must be admitted that such an example exactly supports Whitehead's contention.

Much has been made above of the 'gap' between sense-experience and the *consciousness* of an object, e.g. a cow. We found that this gap might be filled by inference, but that such an explanation was implausible. In considering the gap, Whitehead discards inference and substitutes what he calls 'symbolic reference'. The coloured shape is *not* data from which to infer a cow. It is the symbol for something already felt as part of process—something in presentation much less vivid than the coloured shape but more deeply based in emotion and experience; i.e. the fact that one occasion follows another and conforms with its predecessor. The coloured shape is not the cow; only causal feeling can make us aware of the cow. The coloured shape is given as a symbol, and the involved sense-experience becomes mixed with the feeling of causal efficacy. When the occasion has passed we are unable to distinguish any gap between our cognisance of the coloured shape and the reception of the cow into consciousness. The occasion is past. It is an objective unity.

It has already been seen that 'contemporaneity' describes two occasions which have no causal connection. Therefore the sensations of colour and shape belong to the present, but the *cow*, the object felt in the mode of causal efficacy, belongs to the past. This agrees with the mechanisms of commonsense and physical science, for the entities which are supposed to convey the sensations, the light-waves, take time to move from the object to our eyes. Here 'object' is used in a dictionary sense rather than that required through the special nature of 'object' in Whitehead's philosophy.

It will be recalled that we were in the act of looking out of the window in the endeavour to relate the objects presented to perception with Whitehead's extensive continuum. The objects not only seem solid, but enduring. They appear to be enjoying Newton's 'equable flow' of time. We now turn to the rôle of time required in Whitehead's continuum.

Like Einstein, but unlike Newton, he needs no 'absolute' time. For him, time is the pattern of occasions, and apart from those there is no actuality in duration. He defines contemporary occasions in terms of their causal independence, and the before-and-after relationship in terms of causal dependence.

Stories have been written about an imagined ability to travel backwards in time. But if time is nothing more than the succession of occasions, each derived from and conforming with its predecessor—if, in other words, time is just a way of regarding the pattern of causality—it is clear that such stories are impossible and time is irreversible. In H. G. Wells's *Time Machine* the characters visit the future. But that presupposes empty or absolute time apart from 'things happening'. Whitehead holds out no hope for time travel.

From the point of view of a particular occasion the universe is a real potentiality. The most general scheme of such potentialities is the extensive continuum. But we cannot avoid the untidy fact that Whitehead's continuum is not continuous, but more like a hayfield, the stalks being the actualities, the occasions. This character applies to temporal as well as to spatial extension. Viewed objectively, the things created (the occasions) are continuous, but the creative process (the formation of an actual entity) is not. Each stage of process occupies the whole duration of an occasion. In homely metaphor, Whitehead's time proceeds by jumps. Any one of the occasions includes in its constitution the enjoyment of a stretch of time. We have seen that pulses or beats of energy were suggested by Max Planck and called *quanta*. That is a convenient way of looking at Whitehead's time. But we know that Whitehead, like Einstein, has no stock of *absolute* time to draw upon; he is not serving out slabs of time like toffee. The only available 'slab' is a process of becoming. It is commonsense to say that a thing 'takes time' in order to become something else. But there is no time for the thing to take. Duration is simply a feature of process, as verticality is one of precipices. This characteristic of process can be abstracted and given a name. The feature of an occasion by virtue of which it has duration is called an 'epoch'. With the qualification proposed in the last paragraph, time is not an unbroken flow, but a succession of epochs, or time-quanta, the nature of which are determined by the occasions that 'fill' them.

We have at last tracked down 'real' time and space in Whitehead. 'Real' time is the duration of some actual occasion, and 'real' space the extension of that occasion. Space and time, in classical physics, are external to the entities that make up the universe. In Whitehead they are internal. Each occasion carries its spacetime as part of itself. There is no 'receptacle' or 'frame of reference' apart from the spatio-temporal relations of the separate occasions.

Thus each stalk in Whitehead's hayfield grows its own quantum of spacetime. Each is 'becoming'. Accordingly each quantum, as part of process, is also 'becoming'. But there is a general mixed-upness in the hayfield; it is, after all, more of a relational complex than an expanse of separated stalks. So the most that can be said for the spacetime of the field as a whole is that it is the sum total of whatever potentialities can arise from the process of becoming.

This does not mean that the extensive continuum is ideal or unreal. It is an expression of real, if general, conditions—a generalization of real potentiality. Anything actual *must* be within the continuum, which is the sum or arch-complex of possible spatio-temporal relations.

'Four-dimensional spacetime continuum' is not an alternative term for 'universe' or 'extension'. It is conceivable that a plane universe could exist in which objects were extended only in length, breadth and time; but as it happens the one we know has a dimension additional to the above, i.e. thickness. We understand by 'spacetime continuum' something that has four dimensions and is continuous. Therefore the expression is of a *mode or form* of extension, just as four-wheeled motor cars are members of a class of vehicles that includes three-wheelers.

We are still engaged in the disconcerting act of looking out of the window and trying to discover Whitehead's continuum. It goes without saying that we can feel its extension. But we may still be unconvinced by the undeniable fact that it looks like a lot of *objects* extended in space, and not a bit like the urgent, hurrying occasions on which Whitehead insists.

The remedy is to recall his theory of perception. Even if the objects we see are, in fact, violently active—a battlefield with shells exploding and buildings falling down—the stage still seems to contain a representation of classical physics in dimensional space. But suddenly there is a flash and a whistle and we have lost a leg. The character of the world around us has changed within a moment; all at once we are painfully and unmistakably involved and implicated.

Our experience of the universe at that moment would not be so aptly described as 'classical physics in dimensional space'. Possibly it could best be described as a world of numbness and shock.

The explanation lies in what has already been said of perception. Causal independence is what is meant by contemporaneity. I look at and have sense-experience of the continuum, and because I am contemporary with my sense-experience the world takes on the form of perfectly passive extension (passive, that is, in relation to myself). But immediately I became involved in the causal pattern, *the spatial mode*, in respect of this region of the continuum is gone. I am perceiving causality, the non-contemporary, and whilst this region might have contained a shell bursting harmlessly in dimensional space ('nothing to do with me') it happens instead to contain causal feeling into which ideas of extension do not enter.

If the experience is one of shell-causing-pain, in the mode of causal efficacy, then the two events, the explosion of the shell and the pain, cannot be contemporary, and have not a merely spatial relationship. But what about those elements of the universe that have precisely that relationship and none other? Would not those elements together comprise the universe 'at a given instant'? And would not their existence imply an absolute time, of comfort to classical physics but confusing both to Einstein and Whitehead? Whitehead's answer is that there is no universal contemporaneity, but each occasion has its own field of contemporaries, i.e. those that are causally independent of it. Such enter experience in the mode of presentational immediacy. Their complex data do not contain any causal relationships between elements, but they reflect certain properties (e.g. geometrical) of the contemporary world. It is the mode of causal efficacy that is usually implied when we talk commonly of experience, i.e. the influence of the immediate past in shaping the present.

It will be recollected that the separated atomistic occasions of process are experienced in the form of 'transmuted feelings'. We never see the whole of a thing. When we see a hayfield it is more in the mode of a continuous object than a lot of stalks. There is a symbol here for the differences between Einstein's universe and the one implied in Whitehead's analysis. For Einstein everything is absolutely continuous and there is no region where nothing exists, neither matter, energy nor geometrical fields. But Whitehead's extensive continuum is made up of units of duration and discontinuity—the stalks of a cosmic cornfield. Thus the *extension* of Whitehead's universe in various dimensions is not actual, but potential. It is a continuity invoked by objectivizing something that is not in itself continuous. As opposed, therefore, to the *real* quantum of space and time with which every occasion is born, a space and time that must share the character of process by displaying relativity, we have in the generalized potential continuum a Whiteheadian equivalent to 'absolute' space. Significantly, and perhaps heretically, Whitehead does not admit that his potential space undergoes any geometrical modification, as required by the 'field' theory of Einstein.

Whitehead's concept of potentiality deserves further brief description. It is a key idea if the peculiar identity of his continuum is to be grasped.

We see a newspaper photograph illustrating, say, the Kremlin, a large building with tall, solid walls. For normal purposes this photograph meets all requirements; it conveys to the newspaper reader that the walls of the Kremlin are solid and extended. But a carping observer might say, 'This is not a picture of walls, because walls are continuous; my reading glass reveals that what pretends to be a continuous surface is really a vast number of little dots.'

It is true that half-tone photographs are built up of dots. The picture so constructed is a discontinuous pattern which the observer can objectify into general aspects of extension. The extensity of the walls, as presented, is not actual, but potential. It is a generalized form of the dots.

The dots themselves can be seen to exemplify another mode of potentiality. Through the magnifying glass of the carping reader it is to be noted that they vary in size and shape owing to coarseness of the newsprint. It would be possible to work out the size and shape of the *average* dot and call this the A-dot. Now every dot can be called a potential A-dot.

These two applications of potentiality are called by Whitehead 'general' and 'real' respectively. The newspaper photograph provides a convenient, if imperfect, allegory. The dots are some of the world's actualities. The extension of the occasions is not actual as are the occasions themselves. It is more of the nature of a possibility—more strictly, of a bundle of possibilities out of many available. (There might have been flags on the roof of the Kremlin different from any in the photograph; someone might have been looking out of a window, etc.) The possibility of the occasions getting extended in a particular way is called 'general'. But we also have the occasion itself, which is always perishing and being replaced. For an occasion the possibilities are more confined; they are 'real' potentialities.

We must imagine that we are almost satisfied by now with the view of Whitehead's continuum observable through our window. But suddenly we are aware that things have moved and changed since we began to notice them. We know that classical mechanics produces familar accounts of the movements and changes; but what of Whitehead's continuum?

In considering the elements of that huge pie, nature, we find two major types of ingredient, namely, things and the relations between them. In the proposition 'Peter is the friend of Paul' there are three elements: Peter, Paul and the relational situation, friendship. But there will be other relational situations between Peter and Paul, and there must also be some basic situation from which the complexities surrounding Peter and Paul start. We know that Whitehead finds the latter in the internal constitution of atomistic occasions, which is a mode of feeling. The building up of complex relational situations from these primitive bases must be what we are wont to call 'change'.

To commonsense, as to science, descriptions of time and space must refer somewhere to the laws of motion that are to operate, or else we would have a framework within which it would be impossible for anything to change. As we know, creativity is at the heart of Whitehead's analysis, and accordingly we might expect his world to display little that would restrict the motions of entities; for there cannot very well be change without some accompanying motion.

It is therefore surprising at first to learn that motion is not a characteristic of the occasion considered as a separate entity, that the capacity to change must be denied such entities, as would, of course, follow a denial of motion.

In the interests of clarity it is sometimes necessary to lean too heavily on the illustrative faculty of language, and although we have hinted before that the actual occasion does not change, we have certainly emphasized that the occasion goes through a transition and attains a unity of feeling before it dies, implying that time passes and change *does* take place. It must now be re-iterated that the single atomistic occasion is incapable of such an adventure, and that the dynamic character of process belongs to *groups* of occasions rather than the single entity. The various stages of development from initial data to unified feeling do occur within the occasion, but they do not succeed each other in time. Each occupies the full duration of an occasion.

Reflection will show that the above follows from the nature of Whitehead's continuum. The only mode under which space and time are *real* is when they are expressed as the relations of a particular occasion. It can be said that the occasion, as far as extension is concerned, is what it is because of its spatio-temporal relations. Therefore it is nonsense to speak of an occasion X as acquiring different relations towards space and time; if *those* relations changed, it would not be X, but a different occasion Y.

But what about the manifest change and motion we see through the window? How does that arise? The answer is that change and motion do not affect the primitive atomistic occasions, but are features of groups of occasions which have become related in a special way. Whitehead gives a molecule as an example. It consists of a group of occasions, all enjoying special relations, and it is extended in space and time. Therefore it may be called a slice, or quantum, of the extensive continuum. The molecular occasions of which it is composed do not change; they only display differences. But the 'historic route' of occasions, which is another way of describing the molecule, gathers new occasions into itself as it is extended in time.

The occasions merely die and are born, and that is the only sort of change or motion to be ascribed to them. It is as if the world-process is always picking up handfuls of unchanging things. Change arises from the fact that each handful is different from the last.

It has always bothered philosophers that change occurs in things that somehow, however altered, remain themselves and in a definite sense the same. An old person is an example as opposed to that person as a baby. Whitehead's solution of this classic problem is ingenious. The person is an historic route of occasions, all enjoying highly individual relationships, including those of spatio-temporality. They are always perishing and arising, but in themselves they do not change; they are merely different from each other. (In this connection, motion, the adoption of new spatio-temporal relations with others, is itself a type of change). Now the fact that the person changes and yet remains the same, is still 'Tom Smith' for fourscore years and ten, is explicable when you take one particular epoch in the historic route and compare it with another. The identity of the person consists of living occasions extended in time: a man, plus a history and a future. The occasions of which he is composed in any one quantum of time are quite static; but they are a contrasting lot among themselves.

'All aesthetic experience,' Whitehead says, 'is feeling arising out of the realization of contrast under identity.' Characteristically he goes on to relate this type of experience to nature as a whole. 'In the physical world, this principle of contrast under an identity expresses itself in the physical law that vibration enters into the ultimate nature of atomic organisms. Vibration is the recurrence of contrast within identity of type. The whole possibility of measurement in the physical world depends on this principle. To measure is to count vibrations.'

4. THE METHOD OF EXTENSIVE ABSTRACTION

Space, whether absolute or relational, is the domain of geometry, and the acceptability of Whitehead's continuum must depend in part on the definitions of geometrical and mathematical entities it is possible to derive from it. If the philosopher should be concerned solely with the data of experience, some account must be given of things which no one has ever seen: points, lines, durationless instants, electrons. Such are not amongst the data of experience, but we can be assured that civilization is concerned with them, often to the point of dubbing them 'reality' at the expense of the world of sensed experience. Yet no one ever handles or touches mathematical abstractions, although profound matters, such as whether a bridge is likely to fall into the river, may depend on them. Does there lurk in this topic a confirmation and justification of the bifurcation of nature—a 'fence' between acts of scientific observation and the unobservable king-pins of geometry and mathematics?

Whitehead tackled this problem in one of his earlier works, *The Principles of Natural Knowledge*, and discussed it again, less technically, in *The Concept of Nature*.

The immediate data of experience are *events*. An event is 'the specific character of a place through a period of time'. (We are dealing here with Whiteheadian material of an early date. He had not yet appropriated those forbidding terms, 'occasion', 'society', 'nexus', etc.)

When we think of events we notice their flavour. We savour them. This is part of their uniqueness. A good term for this quality of events is 'specific character'. Whitehead, even at this early stage working characteristically, extends the use of 'event'. Within the useage he adopts, a tree growing in a particular spot for a number of years, or a leaf falling from it, can both properly be termed 'an event'. The content of experience is made up of events in this extended use of the word, including the objects, or specific characters, realized in them.

There is a fundamental relationship between events, i.e. that of extension, or 'extending over'. Whitehead usually symbolizes this by the letter K. Event a extends over event b, or in logical shorthand, aKb, when b is wholly included within a. Thus, if event a is a poet standing on Westminster Bridge from 8 a.m. until 8.15 a.m., and event b is the poet's hand resting on the parapet from 8.5 until 8.10, aKb.

The relation K has various properties. It is 'non-symmetrical'; we cannot have both aKb and bKa. It is 'transitive'; if aKb and bKc, then AKc. Every event extends over other events and is itself extended over by others (i.e. our experience does not contain *either* a vast, all-inclusive world-event extending over all others, *or* electronic events of the smallest possible extent). If a and b are any two events, then there is a third event which extends over both.

Obviously the relation of 'extending over' does not hold be-tween any two events chosen at random, e.g. the Battle of Water-loo and the Battle of Britain. But we can choose a set or class of events such that K holds between any two members. Whitehead calls such a group of events an 'abstractive set', if (i) of any two of its members one extends over the others, if (ii) there is no event which is extended over by every member of the set. This second condition means that there is no least event in the set, since in that case there would be some lesser event, outside the set, which it and all the others extended over. Thus an abstractive set is like a nest of Chinese boxes, one inside the other, except that there is no limiting event corresponding with the smallest box. The systematic use of these abstractive sets defines the nature of conceptual entities, including those of the abstract sciences, without doing violence to the concept of actuality being confined to the event.

It has been objected that an abstractive set has no least term, that there is no smallest 'box' to end the series. Commonsense seems to demand in all things a least term or smallest entity. To this point Whitehead does not appear to offer an answer.

CHAPTER FIVE

GOD

―――――

1. RELIGION IN THE MAKING

Any modest approval or popularity of Whitehead as a philosopher is a fairly new development. There is no concealing the fact that the monolithic character of his philosophy can be at odds with an age such as ours, wherein scepticism may be said to be highly respectable; and it seems that the character mentioned is still not effectively diminished by Whitehead's specific efforts to insist that nothing final or dogmatic is being advanced.

Much contemporary coolness towards Whitehead owes itself to the opposition of other, greatly influential, schools of thought. But a portion is obviously attributable to his project—unforgivable to the agnosticism of many modern philosophers—of speculating about God, as if the deity were as accessible to reason as any problem of mathematics. Moreover, God is given *necessity*. He is required as the crown or summit of the structure suggested by Whitehead's analysis of experience with a necessity similar to that enjoyed by Plato's demiurge. On present-day standards this is heresy indeed; for if the philosophy of organism is to be taken as a metaphysical interpretation of experience and nothing more (the '*as if*'), a postulated God seems to amount to unwarranted objectivity (the '*there is*'). God, defined and put in place, is an unfashionable achievement for a twentieth-century philosopher.

It is not intended here to do more than expound, and even within that limitation we propose to touch only the widest aspects of this complex presentation of Whitehead's.

How do succeeding generations justify faith and belief? Each generation, says Whitehead, has to answer such a question, for a peculiarity of religion is that people are always changing their attitudes towards it. All degrees of enthusiasm and apathy come and go. Nineteenth-century conformism and the relative indifferentism of our own industrial society are phases in the long-lived fact that mankind has a religious life.

Since the earliest times the individual has felt himself a prisoner in his own body. It has become profitable, thanks to Dr Rhine's work in paranormal phenomena, to speculate about telepathy. Stories have been written of imagined mutations in the human type, leading to the emergence of thought-readers. It is probable that Whitehead would see such a world as inimical to religion, for he repeats that *religion is what the individual does with his own solitariness*. This idea of *solitude* as basic to religion is undoubtedly important. If this is true, Whitehead is correct in emphasizing that religion is not primarily a social fact. It is the '. . . force of belief cleansing the inward parts . . . A system of general truths which have the effect of transforming character when they are sincerely held and vividly apprehended . . . Religion is the art and theory of the internal life of man, so far as it depends on the man himself and on what is permanent in the nature of things.'

What religion is Whitehead talking about? Buddhism? Christianity? Neither these nor any other in particular. He regards all rituals, bibles and codes as expedient. He does not even consider religion to be *good* necessarily : the god worshipped could well be evil.

Whitehead names four features of the history of religion : ritual, emotion, belief and rationalization.

Ritual is the habitual performance of actions which have no direct bearing on survival. It is essential for a primitive man to hunt for food and water : it is not essential for him to dance. The satisfactions to be got from dancing butter no parsnips. Yet even birds seem to show this instinct for making rhythmical patterns; one has only to watch the evening swallows. They are certainly not searching for food, killing their rivals or courting their mates. They appear to be enjoying a ritual.

Emotion waits closely on ritual. The most obvious way to arouse emotion is to repeat something *ad lib.*

The effectiveness of repetition for arousing emotion must once have been a discovery. Sooner or later ritual must have been elaborated into a system for exciting emotion for its own sake. The way was set for the bull ring and the football game; for ritual and emotion are held to be social phenomena.

To revert to the evening swallows: if their wheelings and cavortings are really a kind of ritual, one might suppose them to obtain satisfaction thereby. Higher in scale one might expect the satisfaction to be more marked, to become a conscious emotion. Whitehead goes back to this primitive consciousness of the emotion derived from ritual to explain the emergence of myth. Men found themselves practising ritual, and the rituals generated emotion. Myth explains the purpose both of ritual and emotion. We are bidden to suppose that the emotions were once enjoyed for their own sakes, as a dog may chase its tail for no ulterior reason. But sooner or later, where consciousness is involved, vacuums must be filled. We are to imagine that the rhythmical movements and percussive noises of primitive tribes were indulged in compulsively. Later it became more clear that the emotions aroused were pleasurable. Soon the ritual was consciously indulged for the sake of the emotion. After that, myth was introduced to reinforce the hidden purpose of ritual, i.e. emotion.

Myth involves a person or thing. There is something to be got out of the person or thing—some advantage, or else a promise not to molest. Thus prayer and incantation are born. If the addressee of prayer is a person, a religion is involved, but if the addressee is a thing, it is not religion, but magic. 'In religion we induce,' says Whitehead, 'in magic we compel.'

At this stage religion is a new formative element in life. As ritual encourages emotion, which is valued for itself, however 'useless' compared with food-getting and survival in general, so religion encourages thoughts.

Thus we have the primitive folk harnessing their emotions to myth and then thinking and elaborating in the religious vein. This is the stage of unco-ordinated beliefs, marked by a curious tolerance. Religion is too young, too close to the primary social fact of ritual; and the idea of fighting for religion, as opposed to the more cogent causes of food, etc., does not occur to anyone.

Whitehead calls the final development the stage of rationalism. The word is used in its pure sense. The age of martyrs dawns, says Whitehead, when religion ceases to be primarily sociable and the note of solitariness is introduced.

We are ourselves at such a stage, and it has lasted for about

6,000 years. The most complete account of the coming of rationalism into religion is contained in the Judeo-Christian Bible. Here we see the reorganization of beliefs and rituals with the aim of making them central to a coherent ordering of life, and the direction of thought and conduct towards some ethically approved purpose.

'The doctrines of rational religion,' Whitehead maintains, 'aim at being that metaphysics which can be derived from the supernatural experience of mankind in its moments of finest insight.' Religion bases itself on but a small selection from the day-to-day experiences of individuals; it relies on the moments of insight, in themselves infrequent and exceptional, or a relatively tiny number. Yet in spite of this limited nature, considered quantitatively as a human preoccupation, it claims universal validity and demands to be applied by faith. In that respect it is something unique in experience, of a different category from all other preoccupations.

Theoretically, one supposes, the rational religion of which Whitehead speaks could have arisen independently of the primitive ritual and emotion from which it is held to have sprung. Whatever the opinion here, it seems fair to assume that a rational religion, introducing the idea of a central ethical authority and the submergence of the self, depends for its appearance upon certain minima amongst a variety of civilizing factors. As Whitehead points out, 'You can only speak of mercy among a people who, in some respects, are already merciful.'

The category of rational religion may be recognized by the growth in importance within a religion of the individual. In primitive times it is the tribe or group which praises, or tries to placate, the person or thing to be invoked. In rational religion the myth, when retained, is reorganized as an account of verifiable historical circumstances. The individual becomes the religious unit; there is personal prayer rather than tribal dance. 'Today,' Whitehead remarks, 'it is not France which goes to heaven but individual Frenchmen.'

Historically, Whitehead considers that rational religion itself *evolves* and assumes varying forms. The religion of the Pentateuch, for instance, was rooted in the idea of racial preservation. 'Such religion,' Whitehead says saltily, 'is a branch of diplomacy.' Within the millenium preceding the birth of Christ the old religions had served their purpose and their work was done. 'They were religions of the average, and the average is at war with the ideal.' World-consciousness appeared, perhaps fostered by the expansion through travel and trade of the boundaries of the known world. New ideas were born, and such were concerned with an essential rightness of things. The will of God was emphasized to a lesser degree than His goodness. By the same token God became increasingly to resemble, not the overlord, but the companion. The reflective books of the Old Testament represent a self-conscious attempt to see these things whole. The note of solitariness is introduced, as in the Book of Job, in an endeavour to find permanence and intelligibility amidst confusion; for no religion which faces facts can minimize evil.

Buddhism regards the personality as the vehicle for evil; and it is necessary, in this view, to escape from individuality. As Whitehead says, [Christianity] ' . . . has always been a religion seeking a metaphysic, in contrast to Buddhism, which is a metaphysic generating a religion.' One virtue of this distinction is that Christianity retains power to develop. It admits that evil is inherent in the world, but bases the admission on alleged historical events. Buddhism starts with the dogma; Christianity with the historical facts.

Religion is founded on three questions of value—of the individual for himself, of individuals for each other, and of the objective world as a whole. Thus the religious idea starts from self-evaluation but ends with a merging of the individual with the rest of the universe. To adopt Whitehead's approach, this final merging must involve occasions of experience failing or succeeding with reference to the ideal relevant to them—a rightness attained or missed. It is a revelation of *character* in occasions in the way that we become aware of character in people. The meaning of harmony is conformity with whatever of rightness there may be in the occasion. Evil is the measure of non-conformity between the rightness and the actualities—the occasions as they are.

The idea of God has received three principal presentations in history: the Asiatic idea, of which Buddhism is the supreme example, involving an impersonal, self-ordering entity, inherent all the time in everything; the Semitic idea, expressed in the Old Testament, which presents God as individual *other* than the universe he overlooks, and lastly the view commonly called

Pantheistic. This involves the God of Asiatic type—impersonal and inherent in all things—but describes the inherence as a phase within the complete fact of the individual identity of God. Christianity may be understood as a compromise between the Asiatic view and that of the Pentateuch, i.e. God is immanent in all things, but at the same time He transcends as Person. The dogma of Person became gradually central to western religion.

People in daily affairs slice the world into various regions for conceptual use and rarely think of the universe as a seamless coat. There is 'art', and some things are not 'art'. There is 'science' and also 'religion'. It is sometimes as if the overalled laboratory worker and the black-coated curate were visitors from separate planets. Yet both rest ultimately on the same realities. The fact that a man has religious feelings is as much a part of nature as the fact that he is made of carbon. In short, both science and religion need some minima of metaphysics.

It is useless to try to discover whether science needs more metaphysics than religion. The only certainty is that a different dosage would be appropriate in each case. Religion cannot rely on the scientific method of 'working hypothesis'. That method involves the acceptance of a proposition as long as it works in practice, and any sign of it not working must lead to the questioning of the proposition. Such amounts to provisional faith, useful in a pragmatic sense. Science can properly rest there; it does not necessarily seek justification or meaning. But these are precisely the quests of a living religion.

Thus whilst both science and religion share the common ground of the universe and must enlist *some* philosophy before the charge can be avoided of preaching nonsense, it is obvious that they have to do with widely differing topics. In a phrase, the topic of science is the prediction and description of experience. It is not equally plain that the topic of religion is God. An atheist with strong moral convictions is religious. Therefore religion might equally be about conduct. Whitehead insists on his idea of solitariness as basic to religion. The occasions add and substract from the common value of the total world; and at the same time they are for themselves their own value. 'They add to the common stock, and yet they suffer alone. The world is a scene of solitariness in community . . . The topic of religion is individuality in community.'

2. GOD, THE ULTIMATE IRRATIONALITY

There are many ways of entertaining the idea of God. You can have a personal revelation; or learn about those of others; or reflect in solitude. Or, like Whitehead, you can engage in analysis of what is experienced and lead yourself by steps, seemingly inexorable, to a limit, or frontier, of rational explanation. It is possible convincingly to refute mediaeval ontologies separately and on merits. Whitehead's arguments are of a different type; they simply represent analyses of experience, and a denial of his idea of God would seem to require the rejection of the rest of the scheme, not because he has produced some formal dialectic, but because the analyses are all in terms of nature. It is not so much like an incomplete syllogism that requires a consequent as a bucket that demands a bottom. For if the universe were in fact the Whiteheadian process, it would follow that there must be some actual entity which has to be taken into account in every occasion but which is itself independent of the duration of an occasion. Such an entity could only be godlike, to say the least.

The wealth of possibility in the universe is truly stupifying. If every actual occasion had access to that wealth the result would be peculiar, yet simple, i.e. nothing would ever happen. The wealth of possibility would leave each occasion indeterminate, and determination is naturally the condition of something happening. The smallest electronic occasion is a limitation upon possibility. So are the actions of men and nations. I am a brick-layer, you are a hotel servant. We could have adopted many occupations; but the fact that we limited the field and chose *one* means that we have an occupation. The alternative of leaving all possibilities indeterminate would have meant *no occupation*. This amounts to order, whilst the opposite implies negation, nothingness. Thus the principle which bestows order, and through order, existence, is a limiting principle. In terms of Whiteheads's scheme it is an actual entity imposing its own unchanged character on every occasion, whereby creative indeterminacy attains its measure of determination.

Thanks to the introduction of the idea of God, we are in a position to attempt description of the sort of universe which would be given to understanding if Whitehead's analysis were to be read as metaphysics—that is, as the description of an objective reality behind appearances. It would consist of the temporal realm—the 'slabs' or quanta of duration—and that realm's formative elements. Beyond that realm and those elements we can know nothing. The formative elements are (a) the creativity by which the occasions display novelty, (b) the 'Eternal Objects', i.e. the well-nigh boundless possibilities for the occasions, and (c) God. Such would be the ingredients of the Whiteheadian universe.

It emerges from the above that God is an 'actual entity' like one of the occasions, although not one that perishes like the rest. To that extent God shares the characteristics of creation. There is no doubt that the occasions, for Whitehead, are primary; his philosophy seems to travel towards a pluralism which stresses their rôle at the expense of the Eternal Objects and God. Thus the account of experience in one of his last books, *Adventures of Ideas,* contains little reference to either.

Nevertheless, it is fair to say that the place of God in White-head's philosophy is at least as essential as wheels to a wheel-barrow. It is untrue to hold that you have built a barrow if you have not provided the wheels. A wheelless barrow could not properly be called a wheelbarrow without qualification. Wheels are not merely an addition to something called a barrow. It is so with the rôle assigned by Whitehead to God.

This implies some important features of God's nature. If one takes the traditional western view, the scene is of the material overlooked by the spiritual. God is not integral to such a system : neither, as St Thomas Aquinas implied, is He self-evident, because it is always possible to be an atheist. In short, in the face of the God presented by western Christianity, it is possible to do without him. In that respect Whitehead's implanting of God is quite different. You can assimilate parts of the Christian account, retaining say the rules of conduct whilst jettisoning God com-pletely, and thenceforth call yourself a humanist. But it is clear that Whitehead intended that his ingredients could not be jettisoned without doing violence to the whole scheme; and this was applicable even more especially to the element introduced as God. Whether the scheme is as internally sufficient in fact as in intent must be for the judgment of Whiteheadian scholars. Doubts are bound to occur. Whitehead himself, in later years, seemed to 'play down' the rôle of God.

The God of western Christianity is all-powerful and all-perfect, a contrast to every imperfection. He cannot be integral to the universe in the mode of wheels to a barrow, because it is not of the nature of such a God to be integrated as of function with something less than Himself. The barrow might need wheels, but to say that wheels need the barrow would be blasphemous.

Accordingly one can do without God and say that barrows without wheels can be sufficient in themselves. To integrate God *absolutely* with the universe, however, is to limit, in some way, God's nature.

That is exactly what Whitehead has done. God is not a self-existing entity outside the universe of His creation. He has made Himself a formative element, and if His functions or essence rise above that, we cannot possibly know anything about the matter.

Is there, then, some creature *above* God, a being more entitled to be called omniscient? Apparently there is none; or at least, Whitehead is silent on the matter; but it may be said that God obeys, in a sense, something greater than Himself, a principle of creativity which is the ultimate principle and the final generalization to be found in Whitehead.

It is impossible to discuss the nature of God without giving some status to an opposing principle. The question arising from human misery on the one hand and God on the other is: Why does He allow it?

Whitehead refuses to make God the deliberate author of evil. Rather he would view Him as the measure of the aesthetic consistency of the world. But as there is a determinism derived from Him in the creative phase of an occasion, evil must be derived from that determinism. Also, although He is exempt from transition into something else and His nature remains constant through change, inconsistency must somehow arise from His consistency and incompletion from His completion.

Evil is instability. There is a purpose in things to avoid the realization of evil. If everyone were a criminal there would be no police, only bands of criminals. It is the instability of criminality that makes police a practical proposition. Similarly it is the instability of evil that creates moral order.

Evil is not the negation or absence of good. Both good and

evil are positive. 'Evil triumphant in its enjoyment,' says Whitehead, 'is so far good in itself.' But among things greater than itself
it is seen as a destructive agent. It is positive and destructive,
whilst good is positive and creative. Thus evil is not evil in itself,
but in the sense that by its presence the world loses forms of
attainment. Apes are not evil, but if mankind went back to ape-
hood, that would be evil. In particular, evil is to be seen in internal
inconsistency and cross-purposes, resulting in a loss to the
social environment.

God's 'purpose', in the meaning of a direction imposed on
creativity, is the attainment of value. There is a self-interest in
every occasion which gives it an emotional tone. In human terms,
the value inherent in the occasion is what the individual life in
a particular instance 'adds up to'. The values of others—the 'not-
self'—enter as propositional feelings, but the actuality of value
is its enjoyment in an occasion. The whole entity which is the
occasion may be described as a self-value. With self-value and
the 'slab' of duration, the occasion is a miniature edition of the
whole universe, both physical and mental. Thus from an objective
point of view the occasion is a mode of creativity, bringing
together the universe; but subjectively it is to be summarized as
the self-value of the occasion itself. The metaphysical puzzle as
to which is the more 'real'—a subjective or objective standpoint
—in consequence receives an answer.

However, it would be a mistake either to anthropomorphize
or idealize creativity. Value does not exist as something apart
from experience; Thou Shalt Not is not a poster pasted on the
sky. 'There is no such thing,' Whitehead maintains, 'as a bare
value'; there are only individual feelings of value. What we mean
by value is the comparability between such feelings.

Without value there would be no occasions and no universe.
For the measure of value is intensiveness. Zero intensiveness
would be a blank, 'the collapse of actuality'. This is again typical
of Whitehead's insistence on the widest possible generality; one
is bidden here to regard the repetitive 'changing' of a molecule,
and the conversion of a St Augustine, as varying degrees of
intensiveness. He hastens to add that 'occasions differ in importance of actuality'.

Thus arises the creative purpose of God. Apart from God, the
ingredients of the universe would be in confusion—the fish

course mixed with the meat—a flux, a nothingness. The aesthetic order of nature is not *incidental*; there is a universe because of the order.

But if God enters as ingredient in every occasion, what of His nature, as understanding might seek Him, *apart* from the world-process? Is He to be imagined as Supreme Being in the Semitic fashion, or the 'divine ground' of some Asiatic religions? Whitehead's God, it must be repeated, fills neither of these rôles. 'There is no entity, not even God, which requires nothing but itself in order to exist.' There *may* be spiritual beings to fit the ideas of them contained in religious accounts; there may be resurrection and immortality. If so, Whitehead is silent about them. The idea of the whole universe conspiring to produce a new creation with each occasion of experience is perhaps enough to get along with !
' . . . The universe exhibits a creativity with infinite freedom, and a realm of forms with infinite possibilities; but . . . this creativity and these forms are together impotent to achieve actuality apart from the completed ideal harmony, which is God.'

However brief, and however unfairly condensed, the above is an attempt to convey in general terms Whitehead's idea of God. But we expect to find accounts of God in the works of saints and mystics rather than mathematical philosophers, and it is easy to hear voices bidding Whitehead stick to his last. We have already made the point that his scheme purports to be all-inclusive; and as for the qualifications of philosophy for the task, Whitehead expressly maintains that there is no such separate function in human nature as a special religious sense. Religious truth, like any other, must come from the highest pitch of intellect; and if it be argued that religion generates emotions which make the quest for God and value different from 'scientific' quests, Whitehead would reply that it is not true to say that we observe best when we are devoid of emotion.

If religion is what the individual does with his solitariness, its expression through dogma is the return from solitariness to society. 'A dogma is the precise enunciation of a general truth, divested so far as possible from particular exemplification.' It adjusts certain abstract ideas, and one is still forced to estimate the status of those ideas. It must *never* be final. It is religious experience disengaged from the fire of experience itself, ready to face the transformations of history. As such it is necessary: religions commit suicide only when they find their inspiration in their dogmas. We propose to touch, briefly, in more particular detail, some aspects of Whitehead's God, and it may be useful to acknowledge, as we are dealing with a natural theism, that the concepts which concern God in Whitehead must correspond in their place with whatever would be serving as dogmas in a sacred theology.

The account of God we have given so far has been couched in the terms adopted for earlier facets of Whitehead's philosophy. It is now necessary to broaden somewhat. In approaching the present topic we are moving into realms of greater generality. Many terms essential for the understanding of an occasion now tend to look like impedimenta.

It will be recalled that of the various facets of those drops of experience, the occasions—whether subject, object, appetition, concrescence or form of definiteness—each occupies the *whole duration* of the occasion. Of the facets we have named, the most general, and the one which characterizes the occasion most typically, is the subjective aim towards the form of definiteness. It is by virtue of this that the occasion is a process of becoming, and through this alone that the universe lives.

But where does the aim towards definiteness come from? To say that it comes from 'process', or is some kind of spontaneous combustion born of activity, is to retreat into circular argument. Similarly it is impossible to hold that the aim is generated by the completed actualities of the universe. *They* are in the past. It is true that they comprise the objective material for the life of an occasion, but they could no more activate that life than a lump of sugar could get itself eaten and digested. It seems to be required that the driving force which is so manifestly 'there' must be traced to sources within the living occasion, and if such be metaphysically impossible—as indeed is the case—a source must be found *outside* the occasion. Such, on the above showing, could only be another occasion, or living actuality, but of an extraordinary kind, i.e. a non-temporal entity, limited in certain respects, but otherwise identifiable with the God of the advanced religions. God is not an appendage to Whitehead's doctrine of occasions, but is essential to the whole idea of an occasion. The smallest electronic occasion could not exist unless it had received from God its aim towards an individual and particular definiteness.

It does not follow, however, from the above that God is the illimitable creator of the universe. God is to be conceived as an imperfect, aboriginal entity by comparison, for example, with the God of Christianity. Whitehead's God, in fact, does not create the universe. which in its actualities is a process of individual *self*-creation. He is like the artist in our earlier illustration, Who does what He can with the paint, canvas and brushes provided; with the added complication that He is in Himself a further example of *self*-creation.

Another way of looking at the metaphysical position would be to see Whitehead's God as Charles I. Charles is not, in himself, the divine principle behind the Right of Kings. He is an aboriginal instance of the principle, and accordingly 'the aboriginal condition which qualifies its action'. Like Charles I, God requires the world in order to function. It is incorrect to imagine Him as 'first cause', just as it is inconceivable that Charles I could have existed in a coherent sense if there had been no subjects for kings to rule.

The word 'aboriginal' introduced above, is repeatedly used by Whitehead. So is 'primordial'. Such words, as applied to God's nature, express the fact that it is limited. In His primordial nature, God's function is to select Eternal Objects for exemplification by the actualities of the universe. In other words, He is the custodian of the world's potentiality. Does this mean that He keeps a sort of celestial filing cabinet? It would be more correct to say that He carries the potentialities within His nature. ' . . . the differentiated relevance of eternal objects to each instance of the creative process requires their conceptual realization in the primordial nature of God.'

The fact that God is a unique example of a *non-temporal* actuality means that Whitehead has somewhere to 'put' those constituents of the scheme which are not in themselves actual, i.e. potentialities. God does not create them; He needs them as much as they need Him. The general pattern-making character of Eternal Objects, discussed above, whereby they can be conceived as sets, is their character in God's conceptual realization. 'Apart from this realization,' says Whitehead, 'there is mere isolation, indistinguishable from nonentity.' This can be taken to imply that God has no existence apart from His realization of the Eternal Objects. He has no residue of being available with which to visit Moses.

Having said all that, it is necessary to qualify. The above is applicable to what Whitehead calls God's 'primordial' nature; but God has a consequent nature, another aspect altogether. More accurately, the 'primordial' nature is an abstraction from the complete nature of God. It seeks intensity, not preservation; it does not love one thing more than another; it does not envisage any scheme transcending intensity; it is concerned with each actuality as it arises. But God is Himself an actual entity, and as such He shares the characteristics of all actualities. This implies that God is also a process of 'becoming', a self-creative entity seeking satisfaction and definiteness through subjective aim. The fact gives rise to what Whitehead calls God's 'consequent' nature. Whitehead likens the fact that God has two natures to the dipolar character of an actual occasion. The 'consequent' nature arises from the physical prehension of actuality, illuminated by the realm of the Eternal Objects. 'His derivative nature is consequent upon the creative advance of the world.'

The divine nature, perhaps unfortunately for Whitehead's later reputation, is one of the most complicated features of his work, and an aspect which can be found technically treated in many books about Whitehead. It is not proposed to enter here into any more detailed exposition. One of the best of the metaphysical expositions is contained in Ivor Leclerc's *Whitehead's Metaphysics,* and there are interesting discussions in Victor Lowe's *Understanding Whitehead.* The remarks in this chapter, even more markedly than elsewhere in the book, are of a piecemeal nature, intended merely to beckon the reader towards sources of treatment more complete.

To sum up, one might say that there is a blind repetition which builds the physical world. There are also illimitable possibilities. If the latter are to enter the world there must be some element in every occasion through which certain things come to be realized. In order to realize a possibility, such an element would have to include within its nature *all the possibilities held conceptually.*

The 'primordial' nature of God is this complete realization of possibility. One might say that this realm is itself a description of God's primordial nature. He is the complete fact which provides the ground for all experience. Nevertheless the Eternal Objects belong no more to God than to any occasion.

God has limitations. He is limited by His goodness. If God were infinite, He would be evil as well as good. Such a fusion would amount to nothingness.

How did God 'happen'? Was He created? Whitehead is not helpful when it comes to such questions; his explanations here are in the broadest of terms. Actuality is to be thought of as an 'accident', i.e. something not predetermined. One is tempted to say that the first accident that ever happened was the emergence of God, that before God there was unlimited creativity (limitless and therefore not actual), and that after God there is limitation and actuality. But such statements would involve an illicit extrapolation of the spatio-temporal world. Whitehead's God, although 'an actual entity like any other', is not in time. It would be misleading to speak of 'before' and 'after' the emergence of God. For Whitehead, God is the ultimate irrationality, in the sense that explanation cannot be pushed back any further than the nature of God.

We have often had cause to repeat that every occasion is determined by its predecessor and determines its successor. If we kept on numbering causes and effects back in time we should come to that puzzling event, the first cause. The event demands its myth or fable, and the Whiteheadian analysis does not absolve thought from this familiar need. Thus, if we follow Whitehead and substitute actual occasions for causes and effects, we must come to an occasion which is not preceded by any other, a 'thing happening' out of nonentity. One is tempted to assert that the thing that happened in that primordial instance was God, and from that one occasion, not determined by any other, arises the duration and process of the universe, and to save ourselves from the charge of illicit extrapolation by saying that the primordial event was beyond time—that by virtue of the event, time itself was indeed born. But the reader who yielded to such a temptation would find little support in Whitehead.

This is a point on which religious orthodoxy might pounce in triumph; for does not *every* attempt to omit revelation from the account of things fail on the matter of first cause? Whitehead puts this somewhat differently. Rational explanation must depend ultimately on a primordial irrationality, which is God. There is no amount of rationality which can avoid that first reference to irrationality. The situation is the same whatever is involved—philosophy, science or a game of poker. Reason finishes at the point where the something becomes the nothing. 'God is not before all creation but with all creation.'

Evil is in God's nature together with all concepts. It is there to be overcome by whatever is good. Each occasion is what it is; its very evil is a stepping-stone to good, the avoidance of destruction. God adds Himself to the occasion: the universe lives on.

God is not a derivative of the world; He is the actual fact from which the other ingredients cannot be separated. He is the harmony by reason of which there is a world, the binding element. 'The consciousness which is individual in us, is universal in Him: the love which is partial in us is all-embracing in Him.'

Let the last words be Whitehead's:

'His purpose is quality of attainment.

'Every act leaves the world with a deeper or a fainter impress of God. He then passes into His next relation to the world with enlarged, or diminished, presentation of ideal values.

'The universe shows us two aspects: on one side it is physically wasting, on the other side it is spiritually ascending. It is thus passing with a slowness, inconceivable in our measures of time, to new creative conditions, amid which the physical world, as we at present know it, will be represented by a ripple barely to be distinguished from nonentity. The present type of order in the world has arisen from an unimaginable past, and it will find its grave in an unimaginable future . . . '

PART TWO

CHAPTER SIX

EXPLANATION AND GENERALIZATION

1.

The most obvious thing to be said about Whitehead's philosophy is that it contains a number of novel ideas. This is not in itself a recommendation, as it would be for science fiction. Philosophy, like pure science, is unconcerned with novelty as such.

Another thing to be noticed is the literary challenge of his philosophy. It is to be suggested in the next chapter that there is, perhaps, a significance to be found in his later books, considered solely as works of art. Be that as it may, it is true that the works in question were written in language of a remarkable obscurity. As a philosopher he certainly enjoyed an astonishing gift of insight, and the more digestible passages of his books are extensively quoted. It seems that the famous obscurity might have arisen from Whitehead's mistrust of language as a medium for metaphysical expression. A mathematician by training, he found an imprecision in dictionary words which often appeared to threaten the structure of meaning.

On the question of the meaning of language, most people might say that we have experiences on the one hand and a system of symbolic noises and signs with which to express the experiences, on the other. But that is open to objection. If language simply mirrors experience by means of symbols it is hard to see how any of our signs and categories can apply to experience *as a whole*. If the function of language is to make noises to 'stand for' situations within experience, then it is puzzling to consider how we can say anything either about the general character or the limitations of experience as such. Some philosophers, notably Wittgenstein, have taken the heroic course of maintaining that anything said about the totality of experience must be meaningless.

Whitehead did not go to such a length. He took the precaution of coining several words and stretching the application of others to express new ideas. As we have seen, one of the coined words is 'prehension' and one of the stretched applications is that of 'feeling', whilst 'appetition', 'satisfaction' and many other words have more exotic duties to perform in Whitehead than on the level of daily speech.

Language is both the instrument and embodiment of thought, and no century has paid more philosophical attention to it than our own. We speak here of language, not so much as a list of words in human use as a set of *ways* of thinking—of the recurrent patterns in which we form sentences, of the built-in metaphors that decorate the structures, and of the categories, or forms of thought, which become second nature in the course of the history of our species. We have suggested in the previous Part that because the ubiquitous human grammar reflects a view of 'simple location', to that extent there is a built-in metaphysical commitment before one even starts to put language to use, and this topic is illustrated below. In certain areas of thought the only way out seems to be the use of mathematics or the making of adaptions in usage on the lines adopted in part by Whitehead. It will be noticed, for instance, that throughout this book we have presented phrases like 'in that occasion' instead of the more common '*on* that occasion'. This is an example of an attempt to avoid a position imposed by language.

The language of primitive cultures is more than a tool for expression: it is an influence for changing things. The spell-binder seeks power by saying appropriate sentences, even when there is nobody listening. Even to know a person's name is widely held to give some sort of power over that person. On the other hand, the attitude to language of an industrialized society is materialistic. Darwin has taught civilization to seek its ancestors in animality, and thus the eloquent periods of poet or professor are accepted quietly enough as complex developments from *cries*—warning shriek, mating call, etc. It is acceptable to most that thought and language evolved themselves strictly for biological purposes, for the efficiency of planning through communication and co-operation. Thus language is an instrument of such practicability for the daily problems of living that it is not particularly suitable for the expression of the fine distinctions proper to metaphysics. This is an objection additional to that arising from the possibility of 'built-in' categories. Everyday speech must be doled out cautiously if the discourse is philosophical, or else the speaker might come to resemble Steinbeck's awkward cowboy who strokes a kitten only to kill it. This was indeed something of the view of Henri Bergson, who held that, whilst the nature of things can be grasped intuitively, it cannot be expressed.

For Whitehead, the philosopher must needs regard language as the clumsiest of instruments. Unlike Bergson, however, he did not despair of language altogether. What he proposed was to remodel it and create a new 'categorical scheme'. But in the end, he tells us, no form of words will express the concepts implicit in his analysis of experience. The words are impotent, 'mutely appealing for the imaginative leap'—a leap which would, presumably, bring us to a Bergsonian intuition.

It is worth recalling again that Whitehead spent his formative years in mathematics and theoretical physics, studies which use symbols instead of literary language. He seems to have taken from them the view that symbols uniquely suit the expression of abstractions. In one of his later writings he speaks of going back to his first love, symbolic logic. A development is envisaged in which logical symbolism will spread over the whole field of abstract thinking, including even aesthetics and theology.

There are two reasons why one might say that ordinary language and thought-patterns are inadequate to philosophy:

(a) Customary forms of speech lead to self-contradiction. It is a favourite pursuit of modern philosophers to show that traditional 'puzzles' are pseudo-problems engendered by inherent contradictions in language, and prone to vanish when we learn to express ourselves properly. Some, like Wittgenstein, have gone far enough to suggest that an ideal language would be one whose users had no temptation to become philosophers. Whitehead was acquainted with discussions of this type. He warns us of the elephant-trap which language digs in the path of knowledge.

(b) We may hold, with Bergson, that apart from any inherent paradox or contradiction, ordinary language is inadequate to philosophy because it cannot express the reality being sought. Whereas the real world, Bergson complained, is essentially a flux, always changing, language compels us to speak of it as a portmanteau filled with static things. The process of change must be referred to as if it were punctuated by stopping-places. We say 'the child becomes the man'. Less violence would be done to reality, even in the limited sense of 'real' envisaged by day-to-day transactions, if we said 'There is becoming from the child to the man.' Outside the hall where the specialist is lecturing, the familiarity of usage forbids such adventures in expression. This is because a fascist-like ruthlessness of purpose is required of language—that of communication between all people in all conceivable circumstances.

Whitehead also holds that the interrelatedness of things is heavily obscured by forms of speech. We have noticed that the subject-predicate form of judgment makes us think of the world as a concourse of independent subjects, each with its group of predicates, pursuing its own development in isolation. The end-less coming into being and perishing of Whitehead's occasions is implicity denied by the subject-predicate form, which displays the built-in pre-requirement of enduring entities underlying change. We say 'the leaf is turning brown', pointing willy-nilly to a supposedly persistent entity, the leaf. For Whitehead, as we know, this form of judgment is a 'high abstraction', a way of thinking essential enough as a metaphor for daily life, but disastrous for people who try to understand his philosophy.

Of course, there is a celebrated difficulty in this type of criticism. In order to hold an opinion, a philosopher must first have been able to philosophize. As his opinion is that language is riddled with built-in contradictions of reality, he must already somehow have been able to compare what he *has* (language) with something he is merely *in search of* (reality). It follows that he must have some power, presumably other than the power of language, with which he has discovered the modicum he 'knows' of the real world. What kind of power? Intuition? Mystic visions?

Whitehead's analysis avoids this difficulty. *In experience we are experiencing the real world.* It is as simple as that. As we know, some of his intellectual ancestors were the British empiri-cists; in their spirit he started with the proposition that nature is what is given in perception through the senses. He attacks the time-honoured dichotomies of sense-experience and thought, perception and feeling.

In those frequent appearances in this book of 'occasion' in its Whiteheadian sense we have often used the full phrase, '*occasion of experience*'. Far from being a prolix or rhetorical adjunct to 'occasion', the word 'experience' places its partner and itself into a context in which distinctions are possible. The Whiteheadian occasion is not the same as the *datum* of experience, which is the basic concept of traditional empricism. It is below the distinction between subject and object; the datum on the other hand, is an object. Essentially, however, Whitehead follows the empiricists in insisting on the importance of experience, and goes further in holding that the view of nature given to reason by experience cannot be adequately expressed in literary language.

The experience-thought/language relationship has interested many besides Whitehead. Could one be defined without reference to the other—exist, even, without the other? The theory that a person has two mutually *exclusive* powers—to experience, and to think about and describe the experience—is implausible. Experiences seem inextricably mixed with the thoughts about them and the words used to describe them. It is difficult to assemble 'thoughts' that display meaning and at the same time a minimum of dependence on anybody's experience.

A die-hard empiricist might argue as follows. Nothing can be said to exist except whatever is given in experience. As Berkeley said, 'To be is to be perceived.' Words are a particular class of sense-data, and when we speak of 'thinking' or 'philosophizing' we mean simply the act of manipulating these, whether as words, signs or symbols, in accordance with rules of grammar, mathematics or logic. Words have a one-to-one relationship with other data, a relationship of 'standing for' or 'referring to'.

The above is true in general, although there are some difficulties about a few apparently irreducible universals and words like 'and' and 'if'. In fact, there are quite a few words which can be used meaningfully although they do not refer to any sense-datum.

But if in general it is *primarily* the function of language to refer to elements in experience, then it is not easy, as we have noted above, to see how we can say anything about experience as a whole, or the relationship between thought and experience. According to the theory we are considering, a group of words forms a meaningful sentence if, and only if, it can be shown to refer to some identifiable state of affairs, i.e. a specific arrangement of sense-data. To lay claim to any meaning it must be capable of being approved or disproved by observation, or at least it must be *possible*, in theory, to produce the affirmation or denial. The statement 'all men are egotists' cannot strictly be proved true or false, since (a) we cannot examine all men, and (b) it would be a major task to demonstrate the objectivity of even the sample it was found possible to examine. Nevertheless, what we *were* able to produce would be supporting evidence for or against, and the original proposition is not, therefore, nonsensical. Now if we cannot make observations about experience *as a whole*, but only on specific objects, what are we to say of the statements we have been making about the relations between experience and thought? They appear meaningful, certainly, but on the lines we have been considering they must be meaningless. The theory has been worked out with relentless honesty by Ludwig Wittgenstein in his *Tractatus Logico-Philosophicus*. He concludes that we can grasp the common structure or form of experience and the statements which express it, but we cannot say what the structure or form *is*. Once we have understood his ideas, he does not shrink from telling us, we will recognize that most of his statements are meaningless. His book is a ladder which, once climbed, is kicked away.

Whitehead is not as ready as Wittgenstein to abandon metaphysics. At the same time he is always aware of language as a plodding medium. His appeal to the reader to take the imaginative leap *beyond what is being said* is somewhat in the spirit of Wittgenstein.

To see the boundaries of thought and experience and discuss their relationships requires that we should be able to express judgment about objects *other* and less fragmentary than daily experience. From such judgments to wider issues, up to cosmological wholes, seems a matter of degree. Nevertheless Wittgenstein's dismissal of such judgments is immensely influential.

If one could ask Whitehead how he justifies his own work, which amounts to a judgment of all experience, the reply might be somewhat as follows. 'My way is in essence that of the scientist who generalizes from limited observations. The difference is that

I make still wider generalizations. I try to make true statements, not only in single fields of study, but in application to the universe as a whole.'

A pious hope? Surely such a method might be valuable in sorting out interrelatedness, but could it possibly teach us anything about experience *as a whole* in its relations with thought and language? In the end is there not some danger of these flights representing such dim editions of truth as to resemble the gift of *The Innocents Abroad* to someone who wants a Baedeker? Generalization from some experiences to others is valid as far as it goes, but when we come to the *relations* between pristine experience and vaguely apprehended wholes—things-in-themselves, God—the generalizations may surely at best only yield myth or fable.

We propose to present on their merits Whitehead's views on the tools at the philosopher's disposal. Meanwhile it may be useful to glance again at some of his efforts to adapt thought and speech. We have noted his attitude towards the subject-predicate form of judgment, which he takes to be the sort of abstraction that can usefully be made for practical purposes; but if it is treated as a metaphysical category there is immediately implied an account of things of a marked inadequacy. Another difficulty in the world-picture emerges, in that it is not easy to see how the statement 'there are many subjects or substances' can *itself* be reduced to subject-predicate form. Some uncompromising thinkers like Spinoza have concluded that there can only be one substance, namely God. Philosophers have been chased by the spectre of substance into tight corners, often of such constriction that it seems necessary to retreat headlong into the denial of multitudinousness and seek the welcoming comfort of monism.

Like Russell, Whitehead concludes that subject-predicate dogmatists have been trapped by the common form of language, a form that nevertheless made this item of logic sufficiently plausible to go unchallenged for 2,000 years. Whitehead maintains that complex situations cannot be reduced to two-term relationships; we must be prepared for multi-term relationships not reducible to anything else.

We have seen some of the consequences of relational logic in considering other aspects of Whitehead. Logic prescribes the forms of metaphysical thinking, and just as subject-predicate logic is reflected in substance-quality systems, so Whitehead's relational logic is mirrored in his own analysis of process.

Thus the occasion of experience is the focus of vast relationships. Unlike traditional 'substance' it is literally nothing apart from these. It not only a subject, but a 'superject', i.e. the product or outcome of its relations.

Again, an occasion does not always feel others directly; often it feels them only to the extent in which they influence others which are so felt. Hence, when description comes to be translated logically into the simplest terms, multi-term relational judgments are required.

Another transformation of traditional logic is needed by Whitehead's 'eternal object', which does not stand in two-termed relationship with a subject but ingresses into, or is realized in, a complex situation. Blue is not simply to be predicated of a flower; it is to be realized in a situation including the flower, the observer, the source of light, the intervening atmosphere and elements of which the list is endless.

2.

Whitehead is an advocate of human reason as a means to knowledge, and we have discussed some of the pitfalls dug by the faculty of language along the various paths. Nevertheless, reason and intuition remain as two classic routes for humankind. In the view of many who hold to the intuitive method, reason gives faulty clues, because the elements with which it deals have to be abstracted, more or less forcibly, from the totality of things. What is worse, the very nature of reason makes this inevitable. Reason may be likened to a sieve of a certain mesh, and the elements of the world to pebbles. Now the sieve will only pass those pebbles which conform to its nature, i.e. the gauge of the mesh. Such ideas are especially prominent in the work of Kant.

Someone hits his thumb with a hammer. The result is a pain. Pain makes us aware acutely of 'matter' or 'substance'. Hammer and thumb, whatever they are, are what ideas are *not*. The hammer is hard and the thumb hurts. You can see them both : you know they are 'there'.

Yet only one thing is more or less clear at the outset—that

'hammer' and 'thumb' symbolize certain experiences which are shared by a lot of people.

The links between a mind and an object—a hammer—are the five senses plus intuitive feelings. The messages delivered are 'sorted out'—presumably by the brain—and the hammer is 'built up'. For the purposes of commonsense the end-product *is* the hammer, i.e. the hammer *is*. It would be possible to fill volumes with hammer-like data by such means. Essentially, however, the situation is of a series of happenings inside the observer caused by something *other*. It is not the series of happenings that is called 'hammer'. If the sense organs were different it could well be imagined that the happenings would be different; but no one would feel justified in maintaining, in such a case, that the thing which caused the happenings would not be the same thing. This suggests that the bodily organs and feelings say little about what the hammer *is*—perhaps nothing is said. No doubt something is present to give rise to the feelings. The degree of connection is a puzzle. In dreams the feelings occur when no source may be said to be 'there'. In short, as we have noted elsewhere, the idea of substance is so troublesome that it has been jettisoned by many philosophers.

Ideas may be jettisoned from time to time, but it is to these that people have to turn for the tools of living. Some are tautologies of the *a priori*. Mathematical systems can be built from postulates; at no stage is it necessary to go to nature, or the evidence of the senses, for confirmation. $2+2$ cannot equal five. Whatever is as mentally self-evident as this is to be found in the world outside.

The bizarre amazes, but true amazement lies in the fact that the universe is not more bizarre than we find it. In spite of the occasionally untidy corners of Einstein's universe, it is easy to imagine a world where effects follow even less slavishly from causes, where the conclusion refuses to pad after the premise and the sum eschews the digits. One wonders why our law-ridden universe was created instead of this other kind. If God is to have a personality, one is often tempted to follow the conclusions of astronomers in the nineteen-thirties and call it a mathematician's. But why not an Edward Lear personality? Why not a godlike Jacques Tati or a supreme being with the traits of a Bob Hope?

Faced with such questions, some philosophers give up the quest for ultimates. Such a surrender is the same as saying that intuitive feelings, in themselves available neither to be proved nor disproved, are the philosopher's sole contact with reality. Reason, in such a case, becomes a tool for refining and defining, the handmaiden of logic, grammar and mathematics.

Since Kant wrote in the eighteenth century, Whitehead's is one of the few attempts to form a speculative scheme of metaphysics. He is fond of affirming his faith in reason. His zeal reverses Kant's criticisms (some of which we have noted earlier above) and drives against the wind of much modern philosophy, including that of his one-time collaborator, Bertrand Russell.

To have faith in reason implies that one believes the orders and connections between ideas to be the same as, or very similar to, the degrees of interrelatedness between the *things* of the external world. Like most beliefs, this can be held against qualifications and exceptions too numerous to mention. It does not mean that what is implied in our idea of a unicorn is that a unicorn must exist. It means that the relations between ideas are *something* like those between the things which gave rise to them, that the connections between objects of thought are mirrored in the physical world, and that when we think within a frame of logic we use the *kind* of symbolism which corresponds nearest with reality. Ideas entertained in minds are obviously not all true; it is enough that the correspondence should be valid in *some* degree. Were this not so it is hard to see how we could have knowledge. The fact that science makes useful machines seems to imply that we have knowledge. That we have knowledge appears to point to *some* correspondence with truth or reality.

Whitehead points out that a self-creative and novel element is present in everything that happens. Reason is found as a part of this spontaneous creativity. It is an aspect of process which also contains the limits imposed by nature upon the theorizing of mankind.

But the product of reason is explanation, and how far can explanation go? We can explain A in terms of B, B in terms of C, and so on to X—the ultimate which responds no more to any attempts at explaining. Is there, as Whitehead puts it, '. . . a limitation for which no reason can be given; for all reason flows from it'?

A falling apple is explained by saying that it is an example of the law of gravitation. This kind of explanation amounts to identifying a thing as something familiar, showing that it is not unique, but a member of some class. It is possible to go further, as Einstein tried to do, by claiming that a rule is itself a particular case of a more general rule. In the end, however, we seem bound, as Whitehead did, to reach some principle of the widest generality—a frontier beyond which explanation boggles.

Perhaps this is true only of *scientific* explanation? Science is concerned with 'how?', not 'why?' The 'how' type of inquiry leads to the discovery of rules and patterns. If there are no other possibilities in explanation, philosophers have rarely been deterred from attempting them, whether it be to show that nature is a logical necessity, or that the natural order is 'really' shaped by the human mind, or that the whole cosmos is the working out of a divine purpose.

Any explanation must rest on at least one unproved assumption. In the above examples, the natures of the human mind and the divine mind simply have to be accepted as data for which no reasons or explanations can be offered.

This 'ultimate irrationality'—a formidable presence, gibbering and capering at the boundary of sense—might be expected to have the effect of stiffening the rationality of philosophers. The business of speculative philosophy, says Whitehead, is to frame a coherent, logical and necessary system of general ideas in terms of which every element in experience can be interpreted. 'Interpretation' means that everything shall be understandable as an instance of some wider generality. The coherence of a scheme implies that the ideas it contains presuppose each other and are less meaningful in isolation. The logical worth of the scheme lies in its self-consistency or freedom from contradictions. Its 'necessity' demands that it shall carry within itself its own warrant of universality. All this amounts to '. . . an essence to the universe, which forbids relationships beyond itself. . . .'

There is more in this than the mere search for general propositions. What a philosopher of Whitehead's stamp is after is a set of basic categories or patterns in terms of which the whole of experience can be expressed. This is how some scientists might define their own activities. But science is departmentalized into the study of 'bits'. Any scientist who thirsts for the big embrace must forswear his department (Whitehead might here point to his own desertion of mathematics) and go in for metaphysics.

The post-Kantean metaphysician is not trying to find indubitable axioms from which to reason in Euclidean fashion: he is seeking the simplest language in which the elements of nature can be expressed. For Democritus the language was of material particles and their movements; for Whitehead it is of temporal occasions and their internal constitution.

How is the search to be conducted? Whitehead suggests hardheaded observation, hand in hand with imagination. The 'true method of discovery' is like an aeroplane, leaving the ground of 'observation', flying through the air of 'imaginative generalization' and landing again to do some more patient observing.

Many think of reason as the calculating part of man, ordering the confusion of ill-assorted fact. But if that is the function of reason it must be the slave of the emotions, for we do not live in a state of calculation so much as one of appetite and feeling.

It is possible to soften the definition to include criticism. From the downtrodden usher in a school of delinquents, reason becomes guide and arbiter. The double function might stand for two kinds of reason, the practical and the theoretical. The latter is what Whitehead refers to when he says, 'The function of Reason is to promote the art of life.' The practical reason displays a certain utilitarian plainness. Immersed in the analyses of facts and impulses, it tends to become a methodology, releasing skills for civilization, yet at the same time encouraging habits of thought which might too easily degenerate into dogma. The *theoretical reason* approaches the confusion with unconcern as to whether its conclusions will suggest a bomb or a babyfood.

It is to the 'pure' theorist that we look for philosophy, but the danger of formalism besets even the theorist; his systems may in time petrify into stasis like dynastic Egypt, 'the state of satisfactory ritual and of satisfied belief'.

For the purposes of Whitehead's philosophy, reason is a disinterested, evolving function of man, concerned of necessity with the practical aims of life, but more vitally with the task of understanding the whole. This type of reason deserves the adjective 'speculative'.

Whitehead does not think that necessity is the mother of invention. Necessity is the mother of expediency, the make-do-

and-mend, not the lasting thing. The introduction of the lasting thing is nearly always a result of theoretical speculation. Wheeled traffic was a necessity when mankind came down from the trees; the wheel followed after an unknown set of millenia; the self-propelling vehicle has only just been invented. This last fulfilment did not come until the species had advanced far enough in its theoretical grasp of nature. The speculative and theoretical period before discovery always finds an emphasis in Whitehead.

The speculative reason is as old as consciousness, because consciousness always has to do with some group of facts. A fact is understandable both as an illustration of the principles which govern it and as an indication of its relation with other facts. When reason remains unsatisfied it is because such a dual understanding is wanting.

The world is full of limited reasons which are successful for practical ends. A chemist might find all the truth he needs in mechanistic materialism, although he may be a devout Roman Catholic outside the laboratory. Newtonian physics provides all the essential calculations for the Sydney Harbour Bridge; the fact that Newton's system has been modified by Einstein's causes no traffic to fall into the sea. You can sail a boat from Greece to Iceland with no navigational background beyond that given in the Ptolemaic cosmography.

The speculative reason seeks the generalizations behind these limited reasons; it aims to rise above the paraphernalia of method that has become identified with them; to co-ordinate not only appearances 'given' in sensation but the latest findings of science. It has no method. Its function is to ride on methods.

Whitehead loves phrases which seem at once obscure and darkly beautiful, but for him work as terms of precision. He refers to the speculative reason as a 'higher appetition'. That is, the lust for things new and better. Mere *repetition* from one occasion to another, with only the smallest amount of novelty, would lead to vacuity and return man to the trees. From the opposite point of view, *anarchy* in the things presented to consciousness would turn men into village idiots and accomplish the same result. The process of living often contains both repetition and anarchy. It also contains creativity, which mitigates repetition, and reason, which controls anarchy.

If the power of the speculative reason be acknowledged, what is required for metaphysics? We have seen that a metaphysician aims at producing a scheme of related ideas which would account, directly or indirectly in its underlying fundamentals, for all the facts of experience from mysticism to cream cheese. But this is a tall order. It seems to demand that the philosopher must know everything in a world where the possibility even of moderate knowledge grows less as the sum of knowledge increases. Civilization is built on a complexity of cells, each occupied by the squatting figure of its specialist. The age of the 'wise man' is past. Leonardo da Vinci was the last of his race, and clearly philosophers must do the best they can without knowing much more than other people.

When the jet engine was invented it was first drawn on paper. The blueprint looked good; the equations balanced. But would it go? The philosopher has a different problem. His engine is the universe, and it is going already. His task is to display it as a special sort of blueprint. Whether a blueprint is mechanical, as in the case of an engine, or logical, as required by science or philosophy, one of the stricter tests it must satisfy is that of cohesion.

Cohesion is asking *why* of a detail and finding the answer in the whole. A Martian arrives in London. He sees a notice at the railway station which says, 'All Tickets must be Shown'. Whatever can this mean? Does the display of tickets cause pleasure? Are they charms to dispel accident and loss? The answer is to be found in a feature of the railway system as a whole: that it is intended to be a *profit-making* system.

Faith in reason should not totter in the face of incoherence. Observers on Mars, without our knowledge, have planted a 'probe' with television cameras and are now watching a game of rugby football being played in England. They want some explanation of what the cameras are recording which will cohere with their general theories of what happens on our planet. The ranges of the cameras are not powerful enough for the Martians to see the ball; it appears that a lot of men in patterned shirts are performing a dance or orgy. The Martians' attention is drawn to the goalposts. They connect these with similarly shaped objects to be seen on the roofs of some nearby houses. Now it is to be imagined that the Martians understand religions notions but have no sporting instincts. They conclude that the game is a religious dance rite and that the buildings with the H-shaped signs are temples.

The roof signs, of course, are television aerials, and their resemblance to rugby goalposts is accidental. The Martians are wildly mistaken. But their guess illustrates cohesion. They are trying to find meanings in the things seen which will lie together in a harmony that excludes the merely arbitrary. This is precisely the nature of the philosopher's faith in reason, a faith widely asserted in spite of the frustrations to which the above fantasy points.

An idea is of significance the more it is related to a corpus—an existing system of ideas which have already been through the relational mill. But there are certain ideas which occur in the guise of isolation and which nobody doubts. A metaphysical scheme must acknowledge these if it is to be of any use. Most are convinced, for instance, that there is some kind of world outside their bodies with which they make contact through feeling and sense, and that there is a meaning, however incomplete or distorted, in statements about that world. Again, it is common to look for a core of identity in objects, as well as in the make-up of the individual, which endures in spite of growth and change.

These are examples of striking and ancient intuitions. Some intuitions are less widely accepted than others. The strength of acceptance depends in the last resort on what the self is. People who depend on intuitions often bluster in their defence and surround them with references taken from regions beyond the intuition itself. The use of such references is proper to reason, but it is of the essence of intuition to know no reasons. It is possible that intuition is most valuable when it comes at the *end* of a reasoning process rather than at the beginning.

Both for commonsense and philosophy the domain of experience seems divided into parts, such as mind and matter, appearance and reality, particular and universal. We have expounded Whitehead's contention that science divides the world into the sensed and the postulated. Set as he is against bifurcation, Whitehead has no objection to considering experience in its separated facets, provided these are acknowledged to be abstractions from the 'seamless coat'.

This is merely to say that philosophy considers many things.

But the *pursuit itself* is a single activity. The task of drawing a coherent scheme is the production of the one out of the many. It is mistaken to suppose that any part of knowledge is impervious to inquiry and must be left to the type of mystical approach. Marxism and behaviourist psychology would agree here with Whitehead, whilst seeking to ground all experience on physical lines. Whitehead, on the other hand, seeks to establish all experience on lines describable as feeling.

The principal products of Whitehead's early academic life were a book on Universal Algebra and his share in the *Principia Mathematica*. Thus it is not surprising to find him proclaiming the virtue of generalization. All knowledge involves generalizing; all constructive thought has as background some general scheme, however imperfect. A garage mechanic, even a navvy wondering how to shift a load, have at beck a world of pre-formulated generalizations in the absence of which action would be impossible. It is the philosopher's business to carry the matter as far as generalization can reach; and it is when he stops short of complete generality and announces his temporary resting place to be the final goal that the 'insoluble' problems of philosophy arise—questions like 'How can mind influence body?' 'How can a thing exist apart from its qualities?' 'How can anything be itself if change is continuous?'

If such are the sort of difficulties left by incompleteness, it must be hoped that a few more pushes towards generality might resolve them. If there is a casualty in the process it is simplicity. There are no grounds for supposing the truth to be simple. The truth about the universe 'boiled down' to the widest possible generalization is still something baffling in its complexity. We should seek simplicity in our generalizings, says Whitehead, but be profoundly suspicious of it.

This brings us to the goal of metaphysics. The value of a scheme lies in its truth. But no one knows, of course, whether it is true; all that is known is that it is coherent, etc. Truth does not strictly come into the picture; if it did, the philosophical scheme would have to present itself as religion and the philosopher as messiah. On the other hand, the elements of the scheme might be seen at work; its principles, as in Whitehead's philosophy, solving long-outstanding problems. Thus the final and sole test of truth must be limited and pragmatic. If however, the value of absolute and incontrovertible truth must be withheld from a scheme, other features of value should still be on offer. There should be a methodology, as with any set of facts. Both theoretical and applied science should be seen to be contained in it and arise from it.

The above, briefly, is the scope of philosophy as Whitehead understands it. How to start? By ennunciating some first principles? Alas! A snag appears at once. The science of number may well be a tautology from $2 + 2 = 4$; the relation between a geometrical system and its axioms may well be one of necessity; but the topic of axiomatic first principles receives from Whitehead a firm repudiation. Principles, 'first' or otherwise, demand gradual verification. The subject-matter of principle, far from being a basic primitive of expression, is likely of all statements to be the most complex. Thus '. . . the accurate expression of the final generalities . . .' are 'the goal of discussion and not its origin'. This goal is a principle or group of principles for which no reason beyond themselves can be given. They lie where the landscape is intuitive.

In spite of some arguments which we have already advanced, it might be urged with justice that philosophy, as defined by Whitehead, is not different in kind from what is termed pure science. Philosophy becomes (a) a continuation of discovery into greater complexity, (b) a marshalling of the end-products of thought, (c) an explanation of the universe, with its stubborn contradictions, as a system having coherent parts.

A difference is there, and it is important. Science is an adventure in piecemeal objectivity. Whilst from the physicists' point of view it is true that less emphasis must nowadays be placed on 'simple location', science still deals with a world 'out there' beyond the subject. It is a spectacular device, and gives us everything we see advertised in the colour magazines, and tells us what to expect from the laws of nature—what a thing measures and weighs and how it may behave in future. Metaphysics, on the other hand, is an attempt to say what experience *is* rather than *is of*. The alcoholic's conviction that he sees pink elephants is as much a part of nature as the psychiatrist's efforts to explain those pachyderms away.

CHAPTER SEVEN

SOME THOUGHTS ON THE WHOLE

1.

The nature of this chapter demands the dropping of the editorial 'we'—so appropriate to the modes of exposition and incidental discussion—in favour of the first person singular. I propose to say what I think about Whitehead's philosophy.

I must confess to enthusiasm about much of what Whitehead has to say. I am not a disciple of Whitehead's. There are people who are thoroughgoing existentialists, dialectical materialists or convinced anti-metaphysicians; it is doubtful whether there are many Whiteheadians in a comparable sense. On the other hand, Whitehead dispenses shafts of illumination which must have their influence, and possibly the effects of his philosophy are destined to increase.

It is perhaps true that more readers at the present day are finding metaphysical studies acceptable, whilst the same a few years ago might have been touched by guilt-feelings about deserting the principle of verification. Professor Ayer's *Language, Truth and Logic* appeared during Whitehead's major philosophical period, and for years afterwards it was a mark of soundness to assert that a statement had no meaning unless it could be verified. 'God is Love' (in practice an unverifiable statement) was an example of the meaningless ones. 'There is a cat in the cupboard' was meaningful, because you could open the door and find, or not find, the cat. Even 'The Moon is made of green cheese' was meaningful, because, in theory, an astronaut could go there and be able to test that unlikely statement. As it is impossible to talk of a reality behind appearances without using statements of the order of 'God is Love', the conclusion was that meaning could not attach itself to metaphysics, which must be defined strictly as nonsense. Since the publication of *Language, Truth and Logic* this view has been considerably refined and qualified, but it remains the ground of an important modern attitude.

The analysis of 'meaningful' into terms of the verifiability or factual significance of a statement or proposition is not beyond criticism; for if it is recognized that a metaphysician, who tries to say something about a reality behind appearances, is claiming to be making a real statement about the universe, a philosopher who requires 'meaning' to be defined on lines of verifiability is making a most comparable claim. The distinction between 'God is Love' statements and 'Cat in Cupboard' statements, on reflection, is seen to be blurred. Philosophers cannot always avoid making the former kind of statement by implication. If the statement 'There is a cat in the cupboard' is factually significant, a further statement is implied which might read 'The world is such that the statement "There is a cat in the cupboard" is factually significant.' But this is an assertion about reality which, on the showing of anti-metaphysical philosophers, must be treated with suspicion.

If it is true that a philosopher who accepts a principle of verification, however modified that principle may be, cannot always avoid making quasi-metaphysical statements, a further criticism of such principles seems to follow. In order to verify 'There is a cat in the cupboard'—indeed, before we can recognize this at all as a meaningful statement—the world in which we operate has to be one in which the cats are authentic and the cupboards undoubted. This means that the world must be believed to contain objects (cats and cupboards) extended in space. A statement like 'The music of Bartok is purple' would not fit at all readily into such a world; but it is clear that the jolt or jar caused by such statements as 'The music of Bartok is purple', owes itself to a departure from linguistic normality. Part One above contained a note on the gearing of language to 'simple location' and pointed out that in all societies grammar is based on assumptions of quality-nailed-to-substance, a 'nothingness' between subject and object, and a solid universe of 'things' extended in space. It seems to follow that whenever a philosopher appeals to a principle of verification he is prejudging an issue. Far from denying the possibility of metaphysics, he has embraced a metaphysical theory *malgre lui,* i.e. the theory that the real world—against which statements must be checked if they are to be accorded meaning—is a world which coincides with the assumptions of grammatical usage.

A moment's thought, and a reference to what has already been said above about this subject, may show that 'simple location' is not of *necessity* the only possible substructure of language; it is merely—and perhaps overwhelmingly—the most convenient. In realms where, in part, it has been given up, such as subatomic physics and relativity, the result is a straining of language to breaking point, so that description has to be taken over by mathematics.

Although it is most unlikely that common languages could have evolved without the assumption of 'simple location', no logical offence is committed in imagining an exception. To that extent analytical philosophy can be accused of basing itself on a biased selection of one out of several possible systems of grammar. Imagine, for example, that platonism had developed into a form acceptable to everyone, even to the extent of affecting common speech. Grammar, in such a case, instead of being based on a theory of 'simple location' might well have allied itself with an analysis of reality derived from Plato, and by the same token it would resemble Whitehead's account. Instead of bits of material separated by space there might have been bits of temporal duration separated by rhythms, pulsations or other intervals; instead of the reactions of objects chemically one with another, there might have been a 'concern with' or 'feeling for' one thing and another; and instead of qualities, each displayed uniquely by an object, there might have been a universal and static world of pure forms from which each object had to borrow, as it were, its garment.

If history had dictated such a direction for human thought, what would have been the position of a philosopher intent upon upholding a principle of verification? He would surely be giving a most platonic account of the world. Doubtless, as at present, there would be people engaged in sorting out the 'meaningful' elements of language. No less than at present, such would be open to the criticism that their search for meaning was being conducted on *a priori* assumptions of what is meaningful. In such conditions one could almost expect to see factual significance allotted to 'The music of Bartok is purple', coupled perhaps with the liberal assurance that 'There is a cat in the cupboard', whilst being a shade too metaphysical for unreserved acceptance, was not *altogether* devoid of meaning.

Science is essentially the counting of sensible effects and their prediction for the future. Philosophy, if it were finally shorn by public opinion of metaphysics, would thenceforth have to assume the rôle of handmaiden to science and confine itself to spelling out the terms of life as far as it is possible to derive them from our primers and dictionaries. The subjective tasting of nature by each one of us could be admitted into the subsequent account of the universe only in its manifold 'public' effects. Thus a political speech, in the scientific account, is waves in the air, and a member of the audience who promptly shoots the speaker is suffering from paranoia. The real thing about the situation—whatever has *really* happened—is an inaccessible subjective event. The cause of the particular effect, the thing that really happened, cannot be postulated in the scientific account. Substitutes for the real thing can be inferred as general principles, based on statistics derived from the past; by such means it can be confirmed that vocal chords capable of just those frequencies would make precisely those waves in the air. That is one 'branch' of science. For the rest of the situation another branch must be brought in. It will be a more recent branch, closer to the bone of what really happened, and therefore operating with less resolution. Its task would be to show that just those waves in the air, intercepted by the eardrums of a person with a certain identifiable type of history, could be inferred as a potent cause of murder.

Thus, if philosophy were shorn of metaphysics its subject-matter must needs be confined to elements which science understands and which are assumed to have the knack of existing and of offering themselves for examination without incurring either distortion or the necessity of reference to other elements (in the above example, sound waves and mental disease in their causal aspects). But interrelatedness involves a subjective world of events which is inaccessible to science because it can neither be publicly observed nor counted. Indeed, the central criticism of metaphysics lies in the charge that it professes knowledge of the inaccessible.

My own position is one of naive opposition to the anti-metaphysicians. Their arguments have the faintly comic disadvantage of not being supported by thought in general. They show the grim determination of food cranks who are convinced that cereals are bad, whilst the world at large goes on eating bread and rice. Despite the statement 'One needs must love the highest . . .' people manifestly do not always love the highest—and with a similar stubbornness go on practicing metaphysics.

Granted that we are allowed this activity, the next things presented are the instrument for the exercise—the speculative reason—and the method of use, i.e. generalization in Shaw's phrase, 'as far as thought can reach'. Whitehead defined rationalism as the hope 'that we fail to find in experience any elements intrinsically incapable of exhibition as examples of general theory'. The definition cannot very well be faulted, but the product of the thing defined could be the universes of Whitehead, Astrology or biblical fundamentalism. We are left with intuition. Discussion, according to Whitehead, is merely for the purpose of disclosing the coherence of basic ideas, their compatibility and the specializations which can be derived from their conjunction. Thus the dialectical mode of discourse is only a tool for 'the conscious realization of metaphysical intuitions'.

For myself, I grant philosophers permission to philosophize, and it does not worry me that intuition lacks a geometry. Philosophy is a part of literature, and shares with literature the rhetorical function of art. It deals with the general nature of the universe as a theme for presentation, whilst science is the trick of annotating selected aspects in their manifestation as recurrences. Science is not so much *verifiable* as a tautology for verifiability. It is part of the fate of the intuitive side of philosophy to offer itself for comparison against the universe of science, which amounts to a testing, point by point, against the recurrences. The other part of the test is the comparison with human experience. Thus, on the one hand, philosophy seeks to tally with an abstraction (science) and on the other, with the incommunicable (experience). It is not a matter for surprise that philosophy is found in association with literature and rhetoric.

It is a respectable scientific 'fact' that experience is incommunicable. This is merely the consequent of contemporary events being causally independent. As far as I know, the only examples of shared experience occur in works of fiction, such as *The*

Corsican Brothers, a romance by the elder Dumas in which a character feels the stab of pain at the instant of his twin brother's slaughter in a duel. It may be that Siamese twins in real life somewhere have shared an immediate experience, but if so I have never heard of such a case. Thus one might wish to qualify Whitehead's well-known statement that 'the elucidation of immediate experience is the sole justification for any thought; and the starting point for thought is the analytic observation of components of this experience'. The qualification would say that the starting point for thought is not analysis, but the isolated observation that immediate experience is incommunicable. I would certainly take such an observation as an indispensable point to be understood at the outset of Whitehead's analysis. The incommunicable, the actuality of feeling, arises and perishes and becomes a fact. Thenceforth art, science, aesthetics and religion can take over.

2.

People who open Whitehead's books for the first time see a strange world in which everything is relational and nothing complete in itself except the fleeting occasion of experience. It is a world in which the Pacific Ocean discovers Cortez; the cinema audience is created afresh a billion times during each performance; and the rivers that Caesar did not cross lie as a dark complex in some corner of being.

Let them be calm! It is not perhaps as strange a world as that drawn up by scientific materialism. There is room for mind and matter, free will and predestination, being and becoming. The significance of no cherished sense-experience is put in question. Nevertheless. I do not find it easy to claim that there is no fence or curtain in Whitehead's philosophy dividing existence into separated modes of 'reality'. In spite of his insistence, for instance, that the feeling-ridden occasion is the unique, the finite, the only entity, it is to be admitted that both the objective datum and the Tom, Dick or Harry who is 'having' the feeling clamour at the doors of sense for a more flattering status than the one allotted by Whitehead. Both datum and subject may be 'enduring objects', or in other words, either Percy Bysshe Shelley or a sack of potatoes. One gathers that they could be seen as prepared ground for the causal transaction which produces feeling, i.e. historic routes—poets and potatoes; although they cannot be known at all except by way of the subjective feelings of other entities. Nevertheless, apart from feeling and immediacy, poor Shelley emerges as little more than an element in a logic. One cannot create last week's poem or climb yesterday's tree.

The abolition of substantial being by philosophers is always hard on the reader. If on the one hand we have Whitehead's assurance that the occasions, of necessity, are to be the sole 'bricks', and on the other we are persuaded that some elements have *some sort of being* apart from the occasions, we cannot be blamed for looking confused. To say that the sort of being allotted is a logical, conceptual or subsistent being is to starve the reader of definiteness. In Whitehead's case, the being allotted to people and things is one imposed on the universe by the limitation he places on possibility. I feel the snowflake, and the experience is an actual entity in the world-process. But both the snowflake and myself were 'prepared ground', and this ground offers only limited possibilities. I could not have been *bruised* by the snowflake; I might have been bruised if it had been a hailstone.

In other words, the subjective form, *how* a datum is to be felt, is part and parcel of an occasion and has no existence, logical or otherwise, outside it. We cannot recapture the emotion created by a phrase of music; we can only try so to arrange events that it is repeated. But that is making do with a new emotion. Where are the snows of yesteryear?

The above, of course, is not the expression of a technical criticism, but merely of a psychological dissatisfaction. The possession of a rounded, continuing being seems to me a prime human requirement. We take satisfaction in ourselves and others as settled facts: we do not fall in love with a society or write odes to a nexus. The dissatisfaction I have noted arises from human need rather than intellectual fulfilment. Scholarly application to Whitehead rarely at first touches the firm path of equilibrium; but one wonders what would happen if this philosophy were widely accepted and taken into consciousness. There is an invitation to vertigo in the point of creative advance. One half imagines the emergence of yet another type of existential anxiety. Whitehead's accounts of what is 'real' and what 'exists' are clear in themselves; in some respects they do not alter the ground of understanding so much as illuminate it. But our understanding, nevertheless, has not been *this* sort of understanding. One feels, in short, that the past has lost some of its identity with the individual to the advantage of the present. I am for ever a dead weight of settled fact hurtling through a pinhole to adventure.

Whatever the doubts of the reader about the diminishment of his being, he is almost bound to admit that there are aspects of experience which appear to gain in clarity by virtue of Whitehead's analysis. The spheres of perception and causation are obvious examples. Another—and one which has not, on the whole, received adequate justice from Whitehead's commentators —is the notion of societies and nexūs. The value of these concepts is not so much metaphysical as analytical in the field of the critique of meaning. Practical instances of their value abound. I think, in particular, of a public debate which occurred in Great Britain a few years ago about the reality of an organization called the Establishment. This was supposed to be a kind of conspiracy to promote conventional behaviour, and its mentors were the Queen and members of certain official institutions and parties; its rewards were patronage and honours and its penalties official ostracism. The question of whether the Establishment 'existed' so engaged the press and television that a London club was opened with that name, and still functions. The arguments were either on the side of 'existence' or 'non-existence'; the assumptions of the debate were not adapted for intermediate shadings. To the one coterie, the Establishment *existed*—meaning that there were 'Establishment types' who met and made decisions in that regard—and to the other, it did not exist, because people, it was alleged, did not make the Establishment sort of decision *qua* Establishment.

Clearly, to inject Whiteheadian terms into this debate would have been to throw much light on the underlying ideas, which, for lack of analysis, were never in the event ventilated; for the arguments as posed had little meaning, and what people should have been asking themselves was not whether the Establishment 'existed', but whether this particular piece of the national life displayed an intensity of social order, and if so, *how much*, to what sinister degree of intensity?

Nevertheless, the difficulty about what exists 'really' and

what exists in some mode less than real, is bound to haunt the unwary reader of Whitehead, no less than for the student of Plato.

Concepts of 'existence' and 'reality' have changed since the middle ages. To the exemplary citizen of the Holy Roman Empire the real was the spiritual; the paraphernalia of the physical world were for him exemplars of dream and illusion. Such thinking identified him with the orthodoxy of his day, and he was dubbed accordingly a 'realist'. It was the holder of opposite views (the 'nominalist' of scholastic philosophy) who eschewed the universal. Intermediate views were also known, e.g. those of Aquinas and Duns Scotus, but today even those who acknowledge deity and profess objectivity in values find the mental climate of Plato unsatisfying. The forms, to which he gave the status of complete reality, are so unequivocal in conception that they demand to be visualized. But they remain nebulous. What do they look like? Where are they? The more one strains after them the more coy they become. True, the religious nature finds no difficulty in imagining the Good as an objective principle—the idea of the will of God gives the requisite basis. But less exalted forms defeat the mind. What is the form of 'the fizzy'? A cosmic syphon of all-perfect soda water? Can the universal of 'succulence' be a heavenly oyster or supernatural beefsteak? The doctrine that every conception of ours is a shadow of some frozen and perfect idea sounds fine in an atmosphere of morals and divinity, but there is little scope in that atmosphere for buttocks, braces or bowlers.

Another difficulty appears in the mode of connection between a particular and the universal it exemplifies. This is like the classic argument about the interaction of mind and body. If I will myself mentally to raise my arm, it was said, and proceeded to raise it, how could the first event have anything to do with the second? For if it be admitted that mind is *non*-material, and that matter, by definition, is *all*-material, it is hard to think that any possible influence or relation can exist between them.

Similarly in the interaction of universals and particulars we have an apparent mixing of complete opposites. In each particular object the platonic doctrine requires qualities of universality, and also the status of being by which it is a unitary object. Two mutually exclusive modes of reality are required to inhere in the same object, as somewhat similarly the modes of mental and

SOME THOUGHTS ON THE WHOLE

physical are needed by Whitehead's actual entities. But in that case the modes must of necessity display a modicum of unity.

When all is said, can we agree that the universe is stratified in such an odd way that the measure of reality to be accorded one stratum is greater or less than another? Is the expression 'x exists in a way, but in a way different from y' anything but nonsense? Of all forms of definiteness 'existence' may be thought to be the most unequivocal; the suggestion of shades of meaning should be repugnant to it.

Many take universals to be exemplifications of the laws of nature, which are statistical. To appreciate this, it is quite useful to conceive of the order of things as a succession of Whiteheadian occasions showing uniformities. The patterns are repeated, similarities recognized and joint names given. To some of the similarities scientists give the status of laws of nature. For example, to all particular occasions of light of a certain wavelength they give the name ultra-violet.

The above is open to the objection (made by Bertrand Russell and others) that at least one universal, i.e. 'similarity' is irreducible. If we are forced to admit one universal, why not the whole lot? But even the 'statistical' definition of universals gives them no status outside the particular; they do not exist at all in any readily understood sense until met with in a particular object, and even then seem to be nothing but our realizations of uniformities between things.

So what is *real*? What *exists*? This I take to be the most important question it is possible to ask after reading Whitehead, and it is of that measure of importance because one of the elements for which existence is vouched is God.

One is enabled these days to be more clear about what is meant by the verb 'to exist' than our grandfathers were; and clarity began with the exile of conceptual realism. Commonsense demands of the world's actualities that they have an identity of their own apart from the knowing mind. If I feel a bit of ice it is because something with the constant quality of what everyone calls 'a bit of ice' is in contact with my body, and if my body, with its sense organs, were absent, the bit of ice would still be 'there'. Commonsense goes no further; it does not extend the status of reality to the objects of other kinds of experience. A handled and seen bit of ice is real; an imagined bit of ice is not.

Conceptual realism maintained that the act of thinking about anything, e.g. a bit of ice, is as much an act of consciousness as the feeling of it with the senses. If the ice in its physically-presented form is 'other' than my sense-experience, the ice in its conceptually-presented form must be 'other' than my mental experience. Things that are merely thought about can be just as 'physical' in their effects as the objects of sensation, for I may well get a cold shiver down my spine through thinking about ice, even if the nearest bit of ice were a thousand miles away. Therefore, said the conceptual realists, objects of thought existed in their own right as definitely as those of sensation.

But it seemed obvious that the reality of the seen-and-touched bit of ice must be different from that of the ice which is merely thought about. What sort of reality could be accorded the purely conceptual object? A bug-eyed monster from Mars can be thought about without any danger of bringing it into existence. Yet the fact that it does not exist cannot mean that we are thinking about *nothing* when we think of monsters, unicorns, hundred-headed hydrae. 'What is it that does not exist?' To such a question the answer can be puzzling, e.g. 'A hundred-headed hydra.'

Bertrand Russell's celebrated theory of descriptions, which forms one of the starting points of the twentieth-century school of Positivism, does much to dispel the confusing possibility of objects of thought (subsistent objects) existing in their own right. It holds that 'existence' can be postulated only of descriptions. A description is usually a phrase beginning with the definite article—'the Chiltern Hundreds', 'the Chancellor of the Exchequer'. If we say 'the hundred-headed hydra does not exist', we really mean this, according to Russell: 'There is no animal c such that "x is hundred-headed and a hydra" is true when x is c, but not otherwise.' From construction such as this it is impossible to produce such verbal traps as 'What is it that does not exist?—the hundred-headed hydra.'

Existence postulated of proper names, in this theory, is logically ungrammatical. 'Graham Greene exists' is a faulty version of 'the author of *The Comedians* exists'. Only in its logical form is it possible to assert truth or falsity of this proposition, i.e. 'There is an entity c such that the statement "x wrote *The Comedians*" is true if x is c and false otherwise; moreover c is Graham Greene.'

I take it that God, in Whitehead's philosophy qualifies for

demonstration as an 'entity c' and that, if He did not write *The Comedians*, He provided the conceptual selectiveness without which this, or any other exercise of mentality, would have been impossible. I assume also that Whitehead's God, in His 'primordial' nature, is *wholly* contained in the premises of the doctrine of concrescence; 'He is that actual entity from which each temporal concrescence receives that initial aim from which its self causation starts.' He is not given the quality of omnipotence. He does not transcend the universe, for Whitehead points out that you can never find a transcendent fact in considering actuality. He has no opposite number, no Satan to contend with. One might be justified in reading His name as a courtesy title, were it not for the indications in Whitehead's writings that a more close identification is intended with the God of the advanced religions. The Whiteheadian God is 'the timeless source of all order' and the subjective form of the feelings derived from Him is of that refreshment and companionship at which religions aim.

It is interesting to compare the Whiteheadian doctrine of God with the claim of his philosophy as a whole to empiricism. The appeal to experience in classical empiricism involved the 'given', and inference was not dispensed with in interpreting what was 'given'. But Whitehead is concerned with what experience *demands*. This characterizes in particular the essential success of his analyses of causation and perception. Part of their success would imply that Whitehead has been able to exhibit self-evidence. Unfortunately the same argument (if indeed it has relevance) could not be applied to God in the sense that widespread experience of religious feelings *demands* that God be said to exist. The argument need go no further than the refutation of St Anselm's ontological principle, in which, it will be recollected, God is defined initially as a Being 'than which no greater can be thought'. The idea of imperfection simply cannot enter such a definition. Therefore, the argument ran, if a Being of this sort existed only in the mind, He would automatically fall down on the definition because He would lack full reality; and how could anything supremely perfect lack that first requirement of perfection, objective existence? Thus, concluded Anselm, it is impossible to entertain the idea of God and at the same time say that He does not exist. To this argument, as I have noted elsewhere, St Thomas Aquinas retorted conclusively: It would be impossible to think the opposite of anything that is self-evident.

The profoundly annoying thing to convinced atheists must be the fact that a philosopher of Whitehead's stamp has produced God, as it were, out of the top hat of rationalism. No comparable disquiet need attend those readers who are already theists, because the limitations of the Whiteheadian God are logical ones, dictated by the initial analysis of experience, and no divine attributes beyond the scope of analysis are expressly precluded: they simply are not postulated. The upshot is that Whitehead's God is available both as a secular and a religious concept. It is possible to treat the whole account of God as an especially Whiteheadian way of describing the logic of his extensive continuum, and this approach was adopted by one of the authors listed in the bibliography below (W. Mays). But I think it doubtful, on the evidence of Whitehead's writings about religion, that he intended, or would have welcomed, the naturalization of his theology. This I believe follows, not from the fact that his doctrine of concrescence seemed to demand theism, but from the immanence of values in his universe, so entirely removed from Kantean ideas, and for that matter, from the instinctive thinking of modern technological life.

I must acknowledge some personal misgivings about Whitehead's vision of value. 'In its solitariness the Spirit asks, What, in the way of value, is the attainment of life? And it can find no such value till it has merged its individual claim with that of the objective universe. Religion is world-loyalty.' It seems to me that Whitehead is urging our point of view to shift from the belief in a fairly imminent human perfectability, so prevalent in his own early manhood, to that of an implicit trust in the *ultimate* rightness of things—a rightness, however, that is immeasurable in any time-scale of ours, and of cold comfort to any brand of faith except the most rigorous. But that is precisely the crisis of faith in our time. If there is an even chance, sooner or later, of nuclear man destroying himself, it is unexciting news that God is 'with all creation' and that all is right with process.

The occasion is launched into freedom, but the freedom is not of the nature of a choice between good and evil, as in Christianity, to be consummated in terms of personal salvation or damnation; it is the prolonged groping of God towards the desired harmonies of an 'unimaginable future'. Man is but a fortuitous example of personal order; the groping is shared with sticks and stones, with the very lightning in the sky. It is a rarified conception, and although the tenets of organized religions are on no points excluded of necessity, a conception in itself unlikely to decrease the notorious talent of mankind for inharmonious behaviour. People who think and act consciously with reference to ideals, apart from those who may be caterpaulted, as it were, into such attitudes by personal crisis, obviously form a minority. Moral judgment more often depends on *quantity* rather than quality; condemnation demands a good measure of depravity before it starts to function. Few feel more than superficially indignant about crime as reported in the press and on television; reactions to the widespread violence of our day are in basis the protests of prospective victims. Aside from such disagreeable prospects, these accounts, for the most part, are received with feelings of deep pleasure, and mass-communicators know this. Moral indignation arises more readily when appeals to sentimentality are involved, as in the cases of offences against the more than especially helpless, e.g. the blind. Such give everyone a taste of virtue. On the other hand, the contemplation of theological sin can be stimulating to the point of extreme pleasure, provided that the sin is fashionable. Lust, at the present time is wildly popular as a topic, whilst the sin of gluttony interests nobody.

Compassion is the most de-energizing of the emotions. *Homo sapiens* is a dangerous species, capable of every enormity up to and including his own extinction. The scientific humanist may well agree with the psalmist that the heart of a man is desperately wicked. Theistic faith does not depend on any ratiocinative operation, a fact which reduces moral argument to a uniquely complicated status. The least that can be said for Whitehead's God, as He appears in the rôle of 'ultimate irrationality' or final generalization, is that He shares with the God of Christianity enough objectivity to clear the impedimenta of subjective ethics, to suggest a basis for interrelation between those impossible neighbours, the real and the ideal.

To humanism it appears that standards of conduct are to be found in the laws and taboos of society and nowhere else: there is nothing, in other words, which could be termed a *moral* law with any greater degree of actuality than, say, the income tax regulations, and no credence is to be given to the story put out

171

by religion that certain laws were revealed in the first place by God. Yet one must agree that it is often brought to the individual that there is a *rightness* in things. On the parallel plane of aesthetics this feeling is even more common; somehow it is *known* that the millions who prefer pop music to Bach are wrong, whilst no amount of critical analysis will quite uncover the reason. Whitehead's answer is to lump the aesthetic and moral values into one concept of harmony, and to hold that the attainment of harmony, more or less, is the aim or appetition of each concrete actuality in the universe.

From such a conception the presence of God follows, not in the rôle of appendage, put there, so to speak, to dole out possibilities for mentality, but as a factor in the coherence of the whole.

The difficulties of accepting Whitehead's God must certainly be grave amongst atheists and agnostics. In particular he falls foul, not only of that modern school which rejects metaphysics, but of a trend in anti-religious thought which goes far beyond the somewhat 'dated' arguments of humanists and agnostics. The latter trend is non-Christian existentialism. The year of Whitehead's death coincided with the upsurge of this type of thinking on the continent of Europe. Undoubtedly, whilst many anti-metaphysical philosophers would depose Whitehead in England and America, it is existentialism which seeks to perform that ceremony on the continent of Europe.

3.

Whatever the attendant dissatisfactions, it seems that God, in Whitehead's philosophy, must nevertheless be accorded the status of living actuality. There is no way out; one cannot give him a merely relational being; and indeed Whitehead is at pains to stress that God is an actual entity. His qualification for actuality is one of function; in other respects He does not intrude. No amount of standing on hilltops and shouting would induce Him to appear, because you cannot share his ability to communicate between time and timelessness. To that extent He resembles the ether of Victorian physics: He has just those qualities which are necessary to explain away difficulties. He is x exhibited as being caused by the cause of x.

This is not to say that there is no God of religion: it is to say

SOME THOUGHTS ON THE WHOLE

that rationality has not produced Him. Whitehead knows this, and having introduced God, demonstrates His irrationality. He seeks support for his metaphysically necessitous introduction of God in the undoubted fact that experience contains religious feelings. But experience also contains feelings of permanence amidst change, and homogeneity amidst relativity. Intuition can be strong, but it is the theistic explanation that is of the greater fragility. Of all questions, *What is the final fact?* seems to call for the most general of answers: to this question, 'God' seems the most particular of replies. To empiricism it is as if a physicist announced that some new particle had been discovered —'the Omegon'—which held together the universe and literally was the cause of everything, but was neither detectable to observation nor to be deduced from the condition of the universe it had caused. As one of his critics complains, Whitehead's God saves, not the world, but the Whiteheadian philosophy.

As Bertrand Russell said of Leibniz's theories, there is nothing to show that Whitehead is wrong or, for that matter, right. Experimentally, Whitehead's relativity theory would yield slightly different results from Einstein's. Since no instruments are delicate enough to detect the differences, it must presumably be an open question whether this side of Whitehead's approach should more properly be called science than philosophy. I think it would be wrong, however, to assert that the cosmological part of his analysis must for ever be regarded as bookshelf metaphysics. It is certainly possible that science might invariably refuse the concepts Whitehead offers. This at least is to be anticipated as long as the ground underlying scientific activity holds good. It does not follow that Whitehead's philosophy can never be of scientific service.

So far I have barely mentioned the most disquietive thing about Whitehead's theology, which is neither more nor less than the abnegation of human freedom. There is much *talk* of freedom —of waves of creation bearing unpredicability on their crests— but it turns out that this creative advance is not a human adventure. It is God's adventure. To that extent, the Whiteheadian universe is less humanistic than Christianity. At least one consequence of the Fall of Man was the inalienable right to salvation or damnation; Whitehead's God, on the other hand, offers the spectacle of unique permanency amidst the deaths of actualities.

There is no chance of God saving any entity except Himself. To this extent, Whitehead's theology resembles eastern religion, especially Buddhism, rather than Christianity.

However, whether we find Whitehead's theological *coda* either disquietive or conventional, it would be unkind to dwell overmuch on any myth-making aspect of his work. His prolonged analysis of process and change, spacetime, causation and teleology should no more be overlooked than his most happy power of using one branch of learning to illuminate another. If he resorts to theistic conclusions in answering the unanswerable, he is in good company. His analysis has left him with an unreconciled dualism between the static world of possibility and the kindling of events. Like Plato before him, he conjures up his godhead and writes *finis*.

Despite the difficulties, it is to be hoped one day that somebody will produce additional technical work on Whitehead's analysis shorn of its theistic metaphysics. Such might shift his 'ultimate irrationality' from the sphere of godhead to that of the Eternal Objects. The scheme would then stand with the possibilities for theism unparticularized. To the familiar analysis implicit in the scientific exploration of nature, it would appear almost in the guise of invitation to a rival adventure.

So limited, Whitehead's analysis would be a refreshing alternative to the scientists' scheme. If anything of original metaphysical status could emerge from the scheme, it would possibly be a proposition of the type envisaged above: *The world is such that the statement x is factually significant*—where x is a description, not of 'simply located' objects, but of Whiteheadian occasions. More generally, I would prefer to think of his philosophy, not primarily as metaphysics, but in the more acceptable guise of guide to the similarities and disparities of statements about experience. In this way of looking at his philosophy, 'simple location' and the doctrine of occasions would appear as modes of application, varying with particular aspects of practical experience, just as physics treats the same categories with the disparate assumptions of 'waves' and 'particles'.

Another justification for stopping short at the Eternal Objects is suggested by the probability that Whitehead's God, both in his primordial and consequent aspects, might well be taken to be a principle hypostasized—and a *limiting* or negative one at that, i.e. the manipulator of potentiality. He is supposed to be in charge of a kind of ration book of possibility, because in His absence the field of possibility would be boundless. Yet it is not easy to see why the rationing of possibility must of necessity be a function of deity: natural selection could be an equally plausible agent.

In another context Whitehead points out that ultimate truth is likely to be of high complexity. Because of this, one is entitled to feel surprised at the relative simplicity of God's 'primordial' function, i.e. the limitation of possibility. Whitehead is not especially helpful on the question of how God came to adopt this rôle. If there was in the first place an absolutely boundless field of possibility—i.e. Miltonic chaos—the mathematics of chance would in any case have assured a measure of limitation in making possibilities actual—and, in fact, at least one possibility would be found to have been caught in the situation in a state of actuality, i.e. Miltonic chaos. If God appeared on the scene to 'take over', He would not, probably on several reasonable counts, have been confronted by boundless possibility. He could have improved the boundlessness, in theory, by ensuring that any actualized Eternal Objects were of the nature of a 'random series', like sweepstake tickets selected by a computer. Yet this is obviously not what Whitehead means.

4.

Having put a personal view, which amounts largely to the expression of misgivings about the theistic part of Whitehead's philosophy, I am ready to be reminded that it *does*, inescapably, contain that part, and accordingly offers itself for evaluation as a whole.

It is apparent that the whole contains a comprehensive cosmology, and that Whitehead wanted the world to accept it. 'In each age of the world distinguished by high activity there will be found at its culmination, and among the agencies leading to that culmination, some profound cosmological outlook, implicitly accepted, impressing its own type upon the current springs of action.' But Whitehead would have wished the acceptance to be of hypothesis rather than dogma. I find much to admire in this.

In spite of the doubts expressed above, the winning character of the hypothesis must be admitted to lie in the admission of value at all levels. This does not mean that the simplest action—a stone rolling downhill—is a party to the blaze and gloom of emotion and beauty, and I believe that it would be easy to read too much 'uplift' into Whitehead and regard him as taking, in all things, what W. S. Gilbert called 'the high aesthetic line'. The point is rather that value is *never absent* than that it is invariably 'high'. 'The generic aim of process is the attainment of importance, in that species and to that extent which in that instance is possible.' It is permissible to secularize a value-system; one merely ignores the values as irrelevant to certain experiments and observations. The permission does not extend to *denying* the values, as is the case with crude materialism. If there is any lesson for the world in this, it must be in terms of human responsibility. 'The subject is responsible for being what it is in virtue of its feelings. It is also derivatively responsible for the consequences of its existence because they flow from its feelings.' Thus the abnegation of human freedom in Whitehead is not complete. The subject, as it were, is granted exercise, if only on the leash of the pre-selected possibilities.

Process is geared in some way to creativity, which is the character of ultimate fact. Many readers take creativity in Whitehead to be a boundless sort of overlord behind God, who is Himself a subservient lord. The position is that God is confined to His own nature, which is that of goodness. He is like a responsible engineer who builds a structure, but one must imagine Him as perpetually rushing to the filing cabinets for *ad hoc* bits of principle and information; and the cabinets contain every possible item, not merely those applicable to the work in hand. This is grand and appealing, if somewhat of a lesser vision than the godhead of the great religions. For myself, I would substitute 'adventure' for creativity as the ultimate character. It might be said that God creates positive goodness from an infinitude of possible adventures; or equally that evolution is the manifestation of a kind of cosmic pragmatism. It is adventurous to have dinosauria, but in the long run unsuccessful.

Clearly Whitehead sees harmony and beauty as the aims of process rather than other qualities. One says 'other' despite the fact—so powerful are Whitehead's generalizations—that it is not easy to name other candidates. 'The teleology of the Universe is directed to the production of Beauty.' One should not define an end in one set of terms and exclude the same terms from the means. This is as simple as saying that no one wins a football trophy by playing golf. Thus we see aesthetic terms entering all stages of Whitehead's process, even to the extent of exhibiting wave-mechanics as a union of repetition and contrast. A thread of happenings 'transmits itself as an element of novelty throughout the avenues of the body. Its sole use to the body is its vivid originality; it is the organ of novelty.' He states explicitly that 'value' is the word he uses for intrinsic reality.

When I first became interested in Whitehead I was suspicious of this overwhelming aestheticism, mindful of *fin de siècle* characters who hold lilies in caricatures by Max Beerbohm. But animadversions of this kind are baseless. The aesthetic quality of awareness is one of emotion, and that is the sole sort of awareness open to the vast majority of creatures. It is only a tiny minority, Man—and a sophisticated fraction of mankind at that—which is capable of objectification shorn to any large extent of emotion. ' . . . the more primitive mode of objectification is via emotional tone, and only in exceptional organisms does objectification, via sensation, supervene with any effectiveness.'

It is perhaps in the concept of beauty itself, rather than the ubiquity of emotion, that one might trace an excessive simplicity in Whitehead. 'Harmony', to my way of thinking, is the richer concept. I would place beauty in the character of a particular intensity of experience, and harmony as more akin to the bread-and-butter of appetition. Harmony, where it emerges, is always out of contrast. I do not think this offends against the Whiteheadian notions. But harmony need not be beautiful.

The necessity of finding in all grades of experience the character of an appetition to harmony can be a thorny one. I think of Nebakov's novel *Lolita*. Nearly everyone would agree that the sexual seduction of children is something which society must avoid at all costs. Yet *Lolita* is essentially a love story. Out of the contrast between social iniquity and the historic identity of an individual, a species of harmony emerges. It is an example of Whitehead's 'rightness attained or missed'—partly attained, mostly missed.

These final generalizations of Whitehead's are the intuitions of a philosopher. A reader who studies and approves the prior analysis might have other views. For example, the doctrine of concrescence could be a manifestation of *love*, and that word would then stand as a term of greater generality than those employed by Whitehead. Love is the multiple engine of destruction in the world. A living organism—Blake's 'invisible worm'—eats and tramples its way through creation towards the object of love, and then kills that object. Love is also uniquely creative.

In despite of the mass of books which have been written on Whitehead's work, it is apparent that something remains to be done in the evaluation of his philosophy. Much of usefulness has been achieved, and the present book does not pretend to any larger status than that of cheer-leader. I would like to add, however, that one aspect of Whitehead has been overlooked. Many have spoken of his obscurity, of the brilliance of bits of him quoted out of context, and of the strange effect of his 'packed' sentences. No writer has discussed his place in the history of literature. I find this surprising, because the books of his Harvard period, from *Science in the Modern World* to *Modes of Thought*, seem to me to constitute collectively one of the considerable works of art produced in the present century. There is a golden quality in writing which springs from deep civilization, and it is to be found in Whitehead. It is the strength of art out of discipline. The confusion of the reader often arises from Whitehead's habit of offering multiple descriptions of concepts. Something is being elaborated, but it is not always apparent that what is being said has been said before in terms entirely different. The reader can rarely be sure whether Whitehead is introducing a new concept or casting a different ray upon the old. But in the books under discussion, Whitehead is not writing science: and does not the multiplicity of description belong truly to art? Indeed, the universality of ideas is to be measured by the devious ways in which they can be invoked. In short, and in spite of difficulties which can be traced to sources quite other than grandiloquence, I find Whitehead's books valuable as sheer writing. His topic is the whole of being, and I cannot think that the theme has been done so much justice elsewhere in this century. If these are strong opinions to apply to the thickets of *Process and Reality*, they are personal ones. I claim no qualification as literary critic. What I am suggesting is that some of the work which remains to be done lies on the side of literary criticism.

There is also the question of practical application, a strange question to ask of philosophy. It would be a pity to end this book without mentioning the possibility of putting Whitehead to good use in the context of technological planning. When he published *Process and Reality* the computer industry was an item in science-fiction; today the complexity of process is no more than a challenge to the sophistication of machines. If anything is to be gained from the analysis of reality in terms of occasions, the machines are there for the experiment.

The evaluation of large projects (cost-benefit analysis) has a sizeable literature, and most of this has to do with the search for an acceptable technique. The difficulties are many, but chiefly two-fold: quantifying 'subjective' elements like smells and views, and avoiding 'double-counting'. An example of the former would be the landscape architecture of a new motorway. An example of 'double-counting' would be to reckon the time of maintenance staff as a debit against the man-hours gained by a motorway; (a true debit would be accident cases in hospital; the maintenance men should be reckoned as a separate category of credit—'employment gains').

To illustrate the methodological needs of cost-benefit analysis the Channel Tunnel would be a good example. The engineering base of the project is the physical science of the nineteenth century. The consequential elements, which determine finally whether we want a tunnel or not, belong essentially to the mid-twentieth century and their disciplines have nothing to do with engineering. They are the 'unphysical' sciences of social psycology and economics, with one or two arts like politics, real-estate appraisal and land-use planning thrown in.

It would be an exciting venture to programme such an analysis in terms of Whiteheadian societies and nexūs. For the first time there would be no logical doubt about what is to be quantified, namely a very large number of groups of events chosen on the criterion of causal connection. The costing part of the exercise would be conventional; the allocation of costs, Whiteheadian— and unconventional indeed.

The Whiteheadian occasion as the currency of programming technology might well lead to new possibilities of scope; but this may be debatable. What is more certain is the growing *moral* promise of Whitehead. In the course of this chapter I have registered a personal dissatisfaction with philosophers who would appear to detract from the assumption of individuality in staking its claim to a rounded, continuing being. It must be admitted today that the main testing ground of such an assumption lies in science itself, and in particular medical science. The transplanting of vital organs places in question the assertion of centuries as to the nature of being. The topic is too wide for discussion in a book of this sort, but it is fitting to end on a note of extended relevance. At present, lay and professional committees are conjoined officially in reconsidering a problem which had supposedly been solved by Descartes. Who would doubt that Whitehead could offer much to such committees, and that the contribution of his philosophy might give an illumination at times too intense for comfort?

SELECT BIBLIOGRAPHY

Books by Alfred North Whitehead
The following comprise the works of Whitehead's Harvard, or 'philosophical' period. Whiteheadian scholars should, of course, be familiar with Whitehead's considerable work prior to 1926. Almost any library will offer a list of these. Mathematical knowledge is demanded of readers of the earlier books, but is not required in those following.

Science and the Modern World, Cambridge, 1926.
Religion in the Making, Cambridge, 1926.
Symbolism: Its Meaning and Effect, Cambridge, 1928.
Process and Reality, Cambridge, 1929.
The Function of Reason, Princeton, 1929.
The Aims of Education and Other Essays, London, 1929.
Adventures of Ideas, Cambridge, 1933.
Modes of Thought, Cambridge, 1938.

Books about Whitehead's philosophy:

Emmet, Dorothy M., *Whitehead's Philosophy of Organism*, London, 1932.
Das, R., *The Philosophy of Whitehead*, London, 1938.
Bowman, A. A., *A Sacramental Universe*, Princeton, 1939.
Blyth, J. W., *Whitehead's Theory of Knowledge*, Brown University, 1941.
Schilpp, P. A., *The Philosophy of Alfred North Whitehead* (Library of Living Philosophers, Vol. 3), Chicago, 1941.
Hammerschmidt, W. W., *Whitehead's Philosophy of Time*, New York, 1947.
Shahan, E. P., *Whitehead's Theory of Experience*, Oxford, 1950.
Wells, H. K., *Process and Unreality*, Oxford, 1950.
Hartshorne, C., *Whitehead and the Modern World* (with A. H. Johnson and Victor Lowe), Boston, 1950.
Northrop, F. S. C., and Gross, Mason W. (eds.), *Alfred North Whitehead: An Anthology*, New York, 1953.
Price, Lucien, *Dialogues of Alfred North Whitehead*, Boston, 1954.
Lawrence, Nathaniel, *Whitehead's Philosophical Development*, Berkeley, 1956.
Russell, Bertrand, *Portraits from Memory*, London, 1956.
Leclerc, Ivor, *Whitehead's Metaphysics*, London, 1958.
Mays, W., *Philosophy of Whitehead*, London, 1959.

Christian, W. A., *An Interpretation of Whitehead's Metaphysics*, New Haven, 1959.

Leclerc, Ivor (ed.), *The Relevance of Whitehead*, London 1961.

Sherburne, Donald W., *A Whiteheadian Aesthetic*, New Haven, 1961.

Lowe, Victor, *Understanding Whitehead*, Baltimore, 1962.

Kline, G. L. (ed.), *Alfred North Whitehead: Essays on His Philosophy*, New Jersey, 1963.

INDEX